The One and Only Bing

The One and Only Bing

Bob Thomas

Grosset & Dunlap
A Filmways Company
Publishers New York

Designed by Marcia Ben-Eli

The Associated Press would like to thank the following companies that produced and distributed the
films of Bing Crosby: Paramount, Columbia, United
Artists, Warner Brothers, Twentieth-Century Fox,
Universal, Metro-Goldwyn-Mayer, and RKO Pictures.

Project Director: Dan Perkes
Supervising Editor: Norm Goldstein
Authors: Bob Thomas
          Mary Campbell
          Norm Goldstein
Photo Editor: Suzanne Vlamis

Contents

Bing tries to pick the winner at the $50,000 Massachusetts Handicap in Boston, 1939.

King Bing portrays a fairy-tale king in "Bing Crosby's Christmas Show," an NBC-TV special, December 1970.

Disguised as a foreign count, Bing sits on a Hollywood movie set.

Leading the Grand Feature Parade of the Apple Blossom Festival at Winchester, Virginia, 1948, Bing enjoys an oversized lollipop.

Bing Crosby as an RCA recording artist, 1949.

A Special Tribute to Bing Crosby

by Bob Hope

When Bing Crosby died at a golf course in Madrid, I lost a partner with whom I've had some of the most delightful moments of my life.

Yet it would be selfish to say that it was my personal loss. It was a great loss to his family and to the entire world.

The whole world loved Bing Crosby with a devotion that not only crossed international boundaries, but erased them.

Bing made the world a single place, and through his music he spoke to it in a language everybody understands—the language of the heart.

We lost the most recognizable voice in the world. He called his singing "groaning." We called it magic.

No matter where you were in the world, because of Bing every Christmas was white. And because we had him with us, it will always somehow seem a little whiter.

Bing may have started out as a singer, but while he was here he did more than sell records. His music spread a kind of joy and happiness that had a label all its own.

Although he was courted by king and common man alike, Bing was a simple man who never cared much about himself. Which made him a minority of one.

The world put Bing Crosby on a pedestal. But somehow I don't think he ever really knew it.

Bing asked the world, "Going My Way?" and we all were. He never said an unkind word about anyone, whether he was on life's fairway or in the rough. And that's one scorecard I'd be proud to sign.

Whether he was singing, joking, or just living, Bing always had fun. And somehow he made all of us say, "Hey, he's right!"

On Friday, October 14, 1977, a heart may have stopped, a voice stilled. But the real melody Bing Crosby sang will linger as long as there's a phonograph to be played...and a heart to be lifted.

A tea break for Bing and Bob Hope on the set of Road to Bali, in which they starred, 1953.

The Birth of a Crooner

Where the blue of the night
Meets the gold of the day,
Someone waits for me.[1]

Memories of the burnished-gold voice rumbled through the minds of millions when the news flashed around the world October 14, 1977, that Bing Crosby had died in Madrid. The recollections mingled with shock and incredulity. Americans in their fifties had known Bing Crosby all their lives. He had joined their families in the early 1930s, cheering Depression sufferers with his sunshiny ballads over the radio. Younger Americans knew him from his variety shows on television and the late-show appearances of his movies.

I'm dreaming of a white Christmas,
Just like the ones I used to know,
Where the treetops glisten,
And children listen
To hear sleigh bells in the snow.[2]

Homesick boys in New Guinea and Anzio heard the song over squawking radios and remembered it all their lives. Families in peacetime gathered around the Christmas tree and listened to Crosby sing wistfully of a holiday far away. No matter how many hundreds of times you listened to the song, it was as fresh and homey as a Currier and Ives print.

Too-ra-loo-ra-loo-ral,
Too-ra-loo-ra-lie,
Too-ra-loo-ra-loo-ral,
Hush now, don't you cry.[3]

Father O'Malley singing the Irish lullaby to old Father Fitzgibbon, who dozes off to dreams of shamrocks and shillelaghs. Bing won an Oscar for that movie. How many other indelible memories he left in his more than sixty movies! Whether he was *The Connecticut Yankee in King Arthur's Court* or the amiable con man forever on the

With a dog in his lap, a youthful Bing enjoys a vacation in Miami Beach, 1932.

Road, he was never less than convincing.

So many pleasurable memories wrapped up in the person of one man. He was always offering a cure for the blues—"Wrap your troubles in dreams, and dream your troubles away," "Sing, you sinners," "How would you like to swing on a star?" He pleased the world with his joyful songs and his buoyant being. It seemed there would always be a Bing Crosby.

He was born, as it turned out, on May 2, 1903. Some claimed the date was 1901. During a time when youth was everything in Hollywood, his studio fudged a year and said his birth was in 1904. Characteristically, Bing shrugged and went along with it. Not until after his death did a priest in Tacoma reveal that parish records indicated the date to be 1903, making him seventy-four when he died.

The name came from Denmark, Crosby meaning "Town of the Cross." On his mother's side, Bing was pure Irish. And in fact, the Crosbys emigrated to Ireland, then to England, finally landing in America in the 1600s. Great-grandfather Nathaniel Crosby sailed from Worcester, Massachusetts, around the Horn to Oregon and helped to found Portland in that state and Olympia, Washington. The Harrigans had traveled to the American Northwest from Ireland. In Tacoma, Catherine Harrigan met Harry Crosby, a bookkeeper, and they were wed. To them were born five boys and two girls, of which the fourth child was Harry Lillis Crosby. He arrived at 1112 North Jay Street, Tacoma, on May 2, 1903 and was christened across the street at St. Patrick's Church. For most of his life, and certainly in his later years, Harry remained steadfast to the Roman Catholic faith.

"Although my mother takes a poor view of luck, the luckiest thing that ever happened to me was being born to the mother and father I was born to, and inheriting the characteristics I inherited from them. My dad was relaxed and casual and believed in living in the present and having a good time. He had a full life and enjoyed himself no matter what happened. In his youth, Dad had sung in amateur Gilbert and Sullivan productions. My mother had a sweet, clear voice. Their shared love of singing helped bring them together."

And so with their children. All the Crosbys sang joyfully around the dinner table and in the parlor. In 1906, the family moved to Spokane in eastern Washington where Harry senior worked as a bookkeeper for a brewery. Spokane was then not far from the frontier, and young Harry grew up in an atmosphere of mining claims and roaring saloons.

Harry was seven when he acquired a new name. A neighbor boy named Valentine Hobart shared Harry's devotion to a newspaper comic in the Sunday section called "The Bingsville Bugle." A leading character in the strip was called Bingo. Harry's playmate gave him the name of Bingo; later it was shortened. The name stuck.

Bing acquired the work ethic at an early age. Besides helping out at home, he picked apples, mowed lawns, scrubbed floors, worked as a lumberjack, and rose before dawn to deliver the *Spokane Spokesman Review*. He had a bright intelligence, but rarely applied himself to acquire more than passing grades in school. He was more interested in football, baseball, basketball, and swimming, his special skill, and his after-school activities presaged a lifetime of preoccupation with sports.

Inspired by the melodies of his home life, Bing took a special interest in singing while still in grammar school. He took part in the musicales, offered his deepening voice to the glee club, sang solo whenever the opportunity arose. Catherine Harrigan Crosby, who had more ambition for her children than had her easy-going husband, sent young Harry to a vocal coach. Happily, the lessons didn't take. America might have lost its premier popular singer to the pedanticism of scales and pear-shaped tones.

Bing Crosby never learned to read music. He was a natural.

In 1917, Bing entered Gonzaga High School, an adjunct to Gonzaga College of Spokane. He rankled under the discipline of the Jesuit fathers, but their teachings bolstered his faith and remained with him. At the time, he seemed more interested in pranks, amateur boxing, and working backstage at the Auditorium Theater. Top performers of Broadway—Willie and Eugene Howard, Eddie Cantor, Gallagher and Shean, Fannie Brice, Al Jolson—came through on the vaudeville circuit to display their artistry to the Washingtonians. Bing watched in awe from the wings, and his special idol was Jolson.

"I'd heard his records, of course, and I knew about his vocal abilities, but his chief attribute was the sort of electricity he generated when he sang. Nobody in those days did that. When he came out and started to sing, he just elevated the audience immediately. Within the first eight bars he had them in the palm of his hand."

For a time Bing sought to imitate the Jolson style, but he soon decided that blackface mammy-singing was not for him.

The evolution of the Crosby style began when he moved on to Gonzaga College and met Alton Rinker. Rinker was an expert musical synthesizer who could take the current rhythms of phonograph stars and convert them for collegiate combos. He helped form the Musicaladers and enlisted freshman Bing Crosby as drummer. Bing bought a set of trap drums on the installment plan and beat them with fervor, if no particular talent. The fact that he could not read music didn't bother his fellow Musicaladers. Neither could they.

The Musicaladers enjoyed a vogue on campus and around Spokane, but the group

Bing wears a scrub uniform as a student at Gonzaga College in Spokane, Washington.

broke up. Bing tried to bear down on his studies. His mother wanted him to be a lawyer, and he tried. But in his third year at Gonzaga, he gave up.

"Mom, I don't want to be a lawyer, it doesn't interest me," Bing told his mother. "I want to sing."

"How can you make a living singing?" Mrs. Crosby asked.

"I don't know, but I'm gonna try. Al Rinker and I are planning to drive down to Los Angeles and try to break into show business."

Mrs. Crosby's protests were unavailing. Bing argued that Al's sister, who billed herself as Mildred Bailey, was doing well as a singer in Los Angeles and might be able to help. Besides, big brother Everett Crosby was selling trucks down there and could provide a loan, if necessary.

So Bing packed his drums into Al Rinker's tin lizzie, and they set out for California in 1925.

Bing was bedazzled by what he saw in Los Angeles. Mildred Bailey was singing in a plush speak-easy, and Bing thought it was the most exciting place he had ever seen. He also enjoyed the taste of the bootleg booze and what it did to release his boyish inhibitions. With Mildred's encouragement and an occasional loan from brother Everett, Bing and Al put together a vaudeville act:

CROSBY AND RINKER
TWO BOYS AND A PIANO
SINGING SONGS IN THEIR OWN WAY

Al played the piano and Bing brushed the snare drums and the cymbal as they sang the hit songs of the day in fast tempo, mangling the lyrics in a syncopated gibberish. They managed to find bookings on the vaudeville circuit at sixty-five dollars a week.

The two boys from Spokane developed a style that impressed Paul Whiteman when they were playing the Metropolitan Theater in Los Angeles. An innovator in popular music, Whiteman had introduced George Gershwin's "Rhapsody in Blue" to the American public and hired Bix Beiderbecke, Tommy and Jimmy Dorsey, Jack and Charlie Teagarden, Henry Busse, Joe Venuti, Frankie Trumbauer and other musical greats to play in his orchestra.

Whiteman sensed a unique quality in Crosby and Rinker, especially in Bing, with his Jolson-like quality of being able to hold an audience with his selling of a song. The bandleader hired the pair at $150 a week.

The Spokane boys joined the Whiteman band at the Tivoli Theater in Chicago. Both sat on the bandstand, Al holding a stringless guitar, Bing clasping a French horn he couldn't play. Whiteman introduced them as "a couple of boys I picked up in a Walla Walla ice cream parlor."

Rinker and Crosby made a hit with Chicago audiences. They repeated in major cities through the Midwest, but when they played the Paramount Theater in New York, the two boys bombed. They seemed headed back to the bush leagues when Whiteman combined them with Harry Barris, a singer-composer whose scat style complemented theirs. While the bandleader toured England, the trio toured vaudeville as Paul Whiteman's Rhythm Boys. The tour was adventuresome, not only because of the highly appreciative audiences, but also because of Bing's didoes with the bottle and dice.

When Whiteman went to Hollywood to make a musical talkie for Universal in 1930, he re-enlisted the Rhythm Boys. Bing was scheduled to sing a big production number in *King of Jazz*, but he couldn't make it. He was in jail.

Crosby had been arrested after his car was rear-ended near the Roosevelt Hotel in Hollywood. His date, who lived at the hotel,

Appearing with Harry Barris and Al Rinker, Bing (left) was one of The Rhthym Boys for Paul Whiteman's band, heard weekly on the CBS Whiteman Hour.

"Mississippi" (Paramount, 1935): Gail Patrick,
Claude Gillingwater, and Bing.

Andy Devine and Bing in "Dr. Rhythm" 1938.

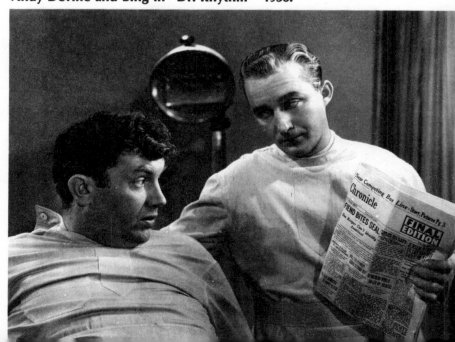

"Pennies from Heaven" (Columbia Pictures, 1936): Bing, making his Columbia Pictures debut, warbles a tune while milking.

"She Loves Me Not" (Paramount, 1934): It's a serious situation for Bing and Kitty Carlisle.

Singing with brothers Bob (top) and Everett (bottom) in 1934, Bing is caught in the middle.

had gone through the windshield. Bing reported to the trial in knickers, brightly colored socks, and sweater, having just finished a round of golf.

"The arresting officer said you had been drinking," remarked the judge.

"Quite," Bing answered casually.

"Are you familiar with the Prohibition laws?"

"Only remotely."

"Thirty days!"

With Bing in the clink, Universal replaced him in the production number with John Boles.

"I have often wondered what might have happened to me if I had sung 'The Song of Dawn' in place of John Boles. It certainly helped him. On the strength of it, he got a lot of pictures after that. I must say, he had a stronger voice and a better delivery for that kind of song than I had. My crooning style wouldn't have been very good for such a number. I might have flopped with the song. I might have been cut out of the picture. I might never have been given another crack at a song in any picture."

The Rhythm Boys made a brief appearance in *King of Jazz* and soon afterward Whiteman bade them farewell with few regrets. The trio appeared in stylish Hollywood places like the Montmartre and the Cocoanut Grove, alternating their jazzy numbers like "Mississippi Mud" with ballads by Bing. One of those most favored by women in the audience was a number Barris had written, "I Surrender, Dear."

Mack Sennett, the wily master of comedy, recognized the power of Bing's style over women. The inventor of the Keystone Kops and other classics of silent comedy was having trouble adjusting to the advent of sound. His gag men thought he had gone loony when he suggested a series of shorts with the little-known Bing Crosby.

"Boys, I admit I never heard of a crooner

E. H. (Buddy) Morris, a New York music publisher and Bing review a song sheet at NBC studios in Hollywood, 1936.

in slapstick comedy," Sennett replied. "But until we flung 'em, nobody ever heard of a custard pie in slapstick comedy. All I know is this boy entertains. And I don't care what people do—they can stand on their heads or count to ten—if they're entertaining, I want 'em. I'm going to sign Crosby."

And he did—at $400 a week, more money than Bing had ever earned before. At first Sennett figured he would need to surround Crosby with expert comics and surefire gags.

Sennett later recalled, "Aside from singing—and we threw in song cues for him on the slightest pretexts—I saw to it that Crosby barely uttered a word. When the first rushes were run off in the screening room, we all discovered instantly what has made hundreds of millions of people happy ever since: Mr. Crosby, with or without benefit of a writer to give him the best lines, was as skillful a comedian as ever stole a scene. He underplayed and made off with every sequence from every comedian we put in his pictures—under the impression we were helping him out."

The success of the Sennett two-reelers, plus a dispute with the operator of the Cocoanut Grove, brought the end of the Rhythm Boys. Harry Barris continued working as a single and turned out more hit songs; Al Rinker became an advertising executive.

Bing's career continued zooming. So much so, in fact, that brother Everett quit selling trucks to manage Bing full time. Everett negotiated a deal with the up-and-coming Columbia Broadcasting System for a series of unsponsored programs at $600 a week. Bing went on the network September 6, 1931, and was an instant hit. Noting that his appeal was equal with men as well as women, Cremo Cigars agreed to sponsor him after the first four weeks. The Paramount Theater in New York signed him for ten weeks at $2,500 a week, and another ten at $4,000.

Bing introduced the radio show as well as his theater appearances with a song he helped write, "Where the Blue of the Night Meets the Gold of the Day." It became recognized throughout America. So did Bing's hit records, "I Surrender, Dear" and "Just One More Chance."

Meanwhile, Bing had gotten married.

For the Love of Dixie

She was born Wilma Wyatt in Harriman, Tennessee, on November 4, 1911. Her family moved to Chicago and Wilma grew into a vivacious blonde who could sing 1920s songs in a cute, bouncy style. She tried out for a blues singing contest sponsored by Ruth Etting and won the competition as well as a new name—Dixie Lee. Miss Etting took the youngster under her wing, showed her how to sell a song, and how to fend off the stage-door Johnnies. Dixie went on the Broadway stage and appeared in the hit musical *Good News*.

Talkies had come to Hollywood, and the studios were scouting the New York theater for handsome performers who could sing and dance. Fox brought Dixie Lee west to make her debut in *Fox Follies of 1929*. Following a good impression on audiences and producers, she was cast in *Happy Days*, *Cheer Up and Smile*, *The Big Party*, *Let's Go Places*, and other breezy musical comedies.

One night a fellow contract player at Fox, Dick Keene, took Dixie to the Cocoanut Grove to hear his friend, Bing Crosby. Bing went gaga over her, as the current expression went. Immediately, he wanted to see her every night. She was intrigued by the ambitious singer, but also wary.

"How can I marry somebody who throws away all the money he makes?" she asked Bing. "Besides, you drink too much."

Bing promised to reform both his fiscal and drinking habits. Dixie was admittedly in love with him, but still she resisted. Her misgivings were supported by her studio advisers.

"Dixie, don't marry that bum," said a Fox boss, Sol Wurtzel. "If you do, you'll have to support him for the rest of your life."

She didn't agree, and on September 29, 1930, Dixie married Bing at the Blessed Sacrament Church on Sunset Boulevard in Hollywood. The headlines seemed to echo Sol Wurtzel's fears:

FOX STAR DIXIE LEE MARRIES SINGER

Bing and Dixie admire their three-week-old son, Gary Evan, in their Hollywood home, July 1933.

Bing clowns at a Los Angeles tennis match, 1935.

Bing gets a pat on the cheek from his wife, Dixie Lee, at a Hollywood restaurant, 1936.

Dixie was earning more money than her new husband, but not for long. She continued in films until 1933, when the Crosbys started their family. Gary Evan arrived on June 25th that year, named for Bing's hunting pal, Gary Cooper. Then came twins Philip Lang and Dennis Michael, on July 13, 1934, followed by a fourth son, Lindsay Harry, January 5, 1938. The Crosbys moved into a spacious house in the San Fernando Valley, then a larger one as the family grew. Dixie at first seemed content with her roles as Mrs. Bing Crosby and mother of their children. Later it was different.

Marriage had a sobering effect on Bing; his days of heavy drinking were over. There was too much work to be done, thanks to Everett. Paramount Studios had been impressed by Bing's sensational appearance at the Paramount Theater in New York, and Everett negotiated a movie contract for five pictures over three years' time. The salary was $300,000.

"If I'm going to get by in pictures, it's going to be as a singer," Bing reasoned, "with about as much acting as you could expect from a guy standing in front of a microphone."

With a reverse switch of the usual actor's ego, Crosby insisted on a contract clause that he would never be starred alone.

"I figure anybody in motion pictures needs plenty of help, cast-wise, and to be associated with good actors and big names with marquee strength. If I let them put 'Bing Crosby' over whatever the name of the picture is, and the rest of the cast in small type, people would say, 'Well, he certainly thinks he's a big shot.' They'd expect greater things from a big shot than I'm able to deliver. If you share your billing with your fellow players, it keeps them happy."

The Big Broadcast was Crosby's first film under the contract, and Paramount loaded the cast with top names from radio: Burns and Allen, Kate Smith, The Mills Brothers, The Boswell Sisters, Cab Calloway, Arthur Tracy (The Street Singer), Donald Novis, Vincent Lopez. It was Bing Crosby that audiences most enjoyed in the movie, and Paramount quickly cast him with Jack Oakie, Richard Arlen, and Burns and Allen in *College Humor*, then with Oakie and Skeets Gallagher in *Too Much Harmony*.

William Randolph Hearst recognized the immense appeal of Bing Crosby and hired him to bolster the sagging career of Marion Davies in a film at Metro-Goldwyn-Mayer, *Going Hollywood*. The movie is little remembered except for the Arthur Freed–Nacio Herb Brown song, "Temptation," but the experience was a revelation to Bing. Miss Davies played the role of movie queen to the hilt, a five-piece orchestra playing tunes to fit her mood. If the mood didn't suit her, there was no shooting that day.

Bing was perplexed. Everett was delighted. Instead of a flat fee, he had negotiated

Bing hunting in the Canadian Rockies.

for Hearst to pay Bing $2,000 a week. Filming dragged on for six months.

Going Hollywood proved a good investment for all concerned. It restored Marion's career, made a lot of money for Hearst, and helped put Bing on the list of the top ten money-making stars in 1934. He would remain there for twenty years, heading the poll from 1944 to 1948.

"Too Much Harmony" (Paramount, 1933):
Skeets Gallagher, Bing, Judith Allen, and Jack
Oakie.

"The Big Broadcast" (Paramount, 1932): Bing
sings with Leila Hyams.

"Going Hollywood" (M-G-M, 1933): Marion Davies and Bing.

"We're Not Dressing" (Paramount, 1934): Bing enjoys a romantic interlude with Carole Lombard, as Ethel Merman looks on.

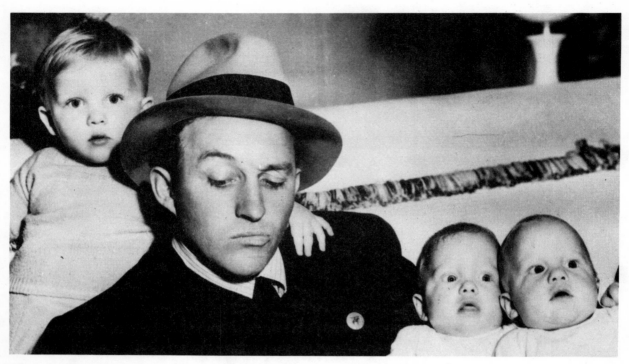

Bing holds the twins Denny, left, and Philip, right, as Gary Evan stands. Hollywood, 1935.

Back to Paramount for *We're Not Dressing* with Carole Lombard, Burns and Allen, and Ethel Merman, then *She Loves Me Not* with Miriam Hopkins.

On *We're Not Dressing*, Bing rebelled. Early in his movie career, he had been warned that he couldn't succeed with his "wingy" ears. True, Jack Oakie had accused Bing of resembling "a whippet in full flight." Paramount had suggested the same remedial operation to flatten the ears that George Raft had endured. But Bing refused. Rather, he submitted to the indignity of having his ears glued back.

One of the scenes in *She Loves Me Not* required heavy lighting. The glue melted and the Crosby ears flapped out like the takeoff of a mallard. When it happened the tenth time, Bing snapped, "This time they're going to stay out."

When the cameraman said that he was instructed to photograph Bing with glued ears, Bing headed for the door. "You can reach me at the Lakeside Golf Club," he said.

Paramount capitulated, and Bing appeared ever afterward with ears akimbo. He also won a victory over heavy makeup. But one discomfort that he could not avoid was the toupee.

Bing's hair began its backward trend before he was thirty. In the pre–Yul Brynner era, no romantic star could have less than a full hairline, so Bing had to submit to what he referred to as a scalp doily or rug. He never liked it, and he perused new scripts to see how many scenes he could play outdoors with a hat. At radio broadcasts and recording sessions, the Crosby hat became standard. When he was head of production at Paramount, Buddy DeSylva promised to buy Bing a script in which he would play a rabbi. "That way you can wear a hat throughout the picture," said DeSylva.

While Bing's movie and radio careers were soaring, his performance on records was helping to revolutionize the music industry.

The early Crosby hits had been released by the Brunswick Record Corporation. Bing became acquainted with the recording manager, a bright, inventive man with an acute ear for popular music, Jack Kapp.

In 1934, Kapp decided to take on the two major record companies, Victor and Columbia, with a new label he called Decca. His first artist was Bing Crosby. On August 8, 1934, Bing recorded a couple of oldies by Carrie Jacobs Bond, "I Love You Truly" and "Just a Wearyin' for You." It was the start of a long and mutually profitable association.

A family picture as Bing poses with wife Dixie and their children in 1938. Children are left to right: Gary, Lindsay, and twins, Philip and Dennis.

Actor Pat O'Brien and Bing chat at the Del Mar, California, racetrack, 1937.

"I can't sing that!" Bing said over and over again to Jack Kapp. "What are you trying to do to me?"

What Jack Kapp was trying to do was establish Bing Crosby as the most popular, as well as the most versatile, recording star in American music. He succeeded in both endeavors. Bing had a modest concept of his own talent, believing himself to be a crooner with a penchant for scat. Kapp banished the jazzy tunes of the Rhythm Boys period and concentrated on a wide variety of songs, from Christmas carols to cowboy tunes.

"Okay, okay, I did 'Adeste Fideles,' but I draw the line at 'Silent Night,' " Bing protested to Kapp. "It's sacrilegious. It'll look like I'm trying to make a buck off religion and Christmas."

Bing's brother Larry, who had come down from Spokane to be his public relations aide, devised a system to funnel profits from "Silent Night" to Christian missions in China. So Bing agreed to record the carol and it became one of Decca's biggest sellers over decades.

Kapp pushed Bing into Hawaiian songs, Stephen Foster melodies, Victor Herbert, barber shop quartets, Brahm's "Lullaby," even the "Star Spangled Banner." However, Bing drew the line at "Ah, Sweet Mystery of Life."

"Absolutely not!" Bing declared. "That's for tired tenors at tea parties."

Kapp did not give up. For three years he continued his campaign until Bing wearied and recorded "Ah, Sweet Mystery of Life." It was a big success, especially in England.

While most singing stars continued a solo path, Kapp continually paired Bing with other performers. Bing recorded with The Boswell Sisters and The Mills Brothers, later with Louis Armstrong, Duke Ellington, Louis Jordan, Judy Garland, Johnny Mercer, The Andrews Sisters, The Merry Macs, The Music Maids, Martha Raye, Harry Owens, and Mary Martin. In 1935 Bing and Dixie performed Jerome Kern's "A Fine Romance" and "The Way You Look Tonight" for Decca. It was their first and only professional appearance together. Dixie then retired completely.

Such was Bing's faith in Jack Kapp that he would not record a song unless Kapp was present in the studio. Kapp traveled from New York to Hollywood five times a year to oversee the Crosby sessions, making an oc-

Bing holds "Sandy" Henville while he sings, 1939.

casional comment. Bing didn't need much coaching; he was a natural. He had a new song played to him once or twice, then tried it in his own style, and finished recording it in an hour.

Bing Crosby records were largely responsible for making Decca one of the Big Three of the record business. Despite munificent offers to join other companies, Bing would not leave Jack Kapp.

"I just did exactly what he told me to do, and it worked," said Bing. "It's a good thing I bumped into him; he was certainly influential in getting me going."

Radio brought Bing Crosby into 20 million homes every week. Oddly, his radio show for Woodbury Soap in 1934 was a failure; the sponsor fired him before the end of the 39-week contract. Woodbury's action remains one of the all time goofs in broadcasting, since in 1935 Bing started with the Kraft Music Hall and reigned as one of radio's top stars for twenty years.

Not that Bing was an immediate radio success. He remained upset about the Woodbury failure and came across uncharacteristically stiff and formal.

"I'm a singer," he told the Kraft Music Hall writer, Carroll Carroll. "Don't give me too many lines to say."

Furthermore, Bing read the lines exactly as Carroll wrote them. No ad libs, none of the easy humor Bing was capable of backstage. Then one day the show's producers conspired with guest star Edward G. Robinson. During one of their dialogues on the air, Robinson suddenly asked, "By the way, Bing, how's your golf score?"

Bing looked blank. He quickly perused his script and saw no line about his golf score. So he responded, "Oh, I'm getting down in the low eighties." He and Robinson continued the exchange, then returned to the script. Later Robinson again threw in an impromptu question and Bing answered casually.

After the broadcast was over, Bing gave one of his rare public displays of temper. The producers tried to convince him that his personality came across much better in the ad lib situation. But Bing didn't like surprises. He finally relented when friends kept telling him how natural the exchange with Eddie Robinson had seemed. Then Bing tolerated an occasional ad lib and he slipped easily into the on-mike casualness that Carroll wrote for him.

It was that easiness that attracted guest stars who normally would not appear on radio shows. These included concert artists like Jascha Heifetz, Gregor Piatigorsky, Rose Bampton, Sergei Rachmaninoff, Yehudi Menuhin, Feodor Chaliapin, Lotte Lehmann. All realized that on Bing's show they could reach a wide audience without demeaning their talents.

At the start of the Kraft Music Hall, Crosby decreed that there would be no studio audience.

"But Bing, how can you play comedy without an audience?" his producer asked.

"The people at home can laugh, if they feel like it," Bing replied. "I don't want a bunch of gawkers."

Again the production minds resorted to trickery. At first a few people from the advertising agency occupied the first two rows of the radio studio. A second row of people appeared the next week, then another. Within a few weeks the seats were filled for the Crosby broadcast. By that time Bing had grown accustomed to working before an audience.

Paramount continued using Bing Crosby as much as he would allow. He starred in three 1935 movies—*Mississippi, Two for Tonight, The Big Broadcast of 1936*—and he made another three in 1936—*Anything Goes, Rhythm on the Range, Pennies from Heaven*, the last for Columbia Pictures. Despite the heavy load, Bing found time for his lifetime passion—sports.

Golf came first on his list of favorites.

"Rhythm on the Range" (Paramount, 1936):
Burns and Bing with animal friends.

"Rhythm on the Range" (Paramount, 1936):
Funny lady Martha Raye (making her movie
debut) with Bing and Bob Burns.

Donald O'Connor, Fred MacMurray, Bing, and friend in "Sing You Sinners", 1938.

"I've been told that I'm relaxed and casual. If I am, I owe a lot of it to golf. Golf has provided relaxation that has kept my batteries recharged when I put too heavy a load on them. It doesn't matter what my professional or personal problems are, when I step onto the first tee I get a sense of release and escape. When I concentrate for three to three-and-a-half hours on trying to play a good game, the studio, my radio hour, and the fact that the latest oil well in which I have invested is spouting water are unimportant."

Bing's devotion to golf was such that he often rose at dawn, walked a block to the Lakeside Country Club, and played nine holes by himself before reporting to the studio. Neither rain nor gloom of night could stay Crosby from his golf game, and fellow Lakeside members often caught the sight of the lone figure carrying his clubs under an umbrella or playing past twilight when he could scarcely see the golf ball. He played consistently in the low seventies. Gene Sarazen, one of the great golf pros, once played a round with Bing and said the singer could win tournaments if he had the time to practice more. In fact, he once qualified in the National Amateur Tournament.

In 1937, Bing started a tradition that has lasted for thirty-nine years: the Bing Crosby National Pro-Am Tournament. It began as a "clambake" get-together at the Rancho Santa Fe course, north of San Diego. In 1947, the tournament was moved to Pebble Beach on the Monterey Peninsula. Bing picked up the tab for all expenses and provided the prize money; any income was donated to charity. His pals from Hollywood flocked to the tournament, and the top professionals made it a must on their annual tours.

In 1935 Bing Crosby bought a horse with the appropriate name of Zombie. It was the start of a long romance with the nags. Soon he was pouring his earnings into the Bing-Lin Stable, which he owned with his close friend Lindsay Howard. The Crosby horses had such a knack for finishing last that they became a prime topic for radio comedians. But Bing was undeterred. He bought stock in the new Santa Anita racetrack, and then he and Pat O'Brien founded the Del Mar track near San Diego in 1937.

"Where the Turf Meets the Surf" was the slogan for the summertime track, and it at-

Actress Mary Pickford and Bing are caught in an offstage moment on a Hollywood set where she was making a movie for the Motion Picture Relief Fund in 1939.

Singing along with Bing is Paul Pettit,
the $100,000 rookie signed by the Pirates.

Bing and three of his sons at the Pirates'
spring training camp in Hollywood, March
1948.

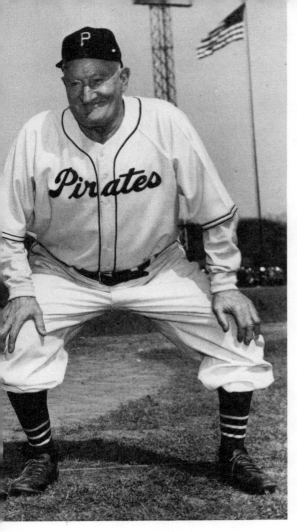

With Pittsburgh Pirates coach Honus Wagner, Bing watches the team practice, 1948.

Vice-president Bing works out with the Pirates, 1951.

With his racehorse, Ligaroti, in Los Angeles, 1938.

tracted the top stars of Hollywood. The pre-opening party was one of the classic entertainments of the year, with Bing, Pat, Mary Martin, Jimmy Durante, Phil Harris, Al Jolson, and others doing their stuff for the select crowd.

Bing also owned an interest in a promising young heavyweight boxer, Georgie Turner, in 1936. Ten years later he was part of a syndicate that bought control of the Pittsburgh Pirates for a reported $2,250,000.

"There's one thing certain," cracked Bob Hope, who often made sport of Bing's losing horses, "Crosby can't hurt the Pirates. They're dead last already."

Youngest son Lindsay is greeted by Bing and Dixie in Hollywood, 1938, following their return from a month's vacation in Bermuda. Son Gary, with his back to the camera, accompanied his parents.

The Road to Happiness

The entertainment world's most famous friendship began on 48th Street in New York City on a warm summer day in 1932.

It happened near the Friars Club, to which both entertainers belonged. Hope had just climbed his way out of vaudeville, and Bing had replaced Rudy Vallee as the singing heartbeat of America. They recognized each other on the street, exchanged a few pleasantries, and went on their ways.

Two months later, fate threw them together on the same bill at the Capitol Theater on Broadway.

"Let's do something together," suggested Hope. "I know an old vaudeville routine that is so corny it's funny."

"Like your jokes?" Crosby said airily.

After Hope told his jokes and Crosby sang his songs, the pair met at center stage and exchanged a few words. Then Hope announced, "We'd like to give you our impression of two farmers meeting on the street."

They went to opposite sides of the stage, then walked to the middle. "How are things?" Hope asked. Crosby turned his thumbs down and Hope milked them.

"Now we'd like to give you our impression of two politicians meeting on the street," said Hope. Again they hailed and approached each other and then started picking each other's pockets!

From that first time at the Capitol Theater, Crosby and Hope went together like Scotch and soda, mustard and hot dogs. By another lucky happenstance, Hope was signed by Paramount Pictures, and the pair renewed their acquaintance around the studio lot.

After Hope's debut in features—he started in *The Big Broadcast of 1938*—the comedian was shunted into B pictures. But his brash style was making him a big star in radio, and he often exchanged guest appearances with Bing.

"The widely publicized Hope-Crosby feud was not a planned vendetta. It grew

It's Bing and Bob Hope under those burnooses for Road to Morocco (Paramount, 1942).

"Rhythm on the River" (Paramount, 1940): Bing and Mary Martin.

"The Star Maker" (Paramount, 1939): Bing and Linda Ware.

Edward Everett Horton, Franciska Gaal, and Bing in "Paris Honeymoon" 1939.

Bing and Shirley Ross in "Waikiki Wedding" 1937.

out of the fact that when we appeared on each other's radio programs and in 'The Road' pictures it seemed easier for our writers to write abusive dialogue than any other kind. When our Hatfield-McCoy routine became a byword with the public, we did nothing to derail it. We developed and expanded it, and pitched in merrily to think of insults to hurl at each other.''

Bob came to the Kraft Music Hall and Bing arrived at the Bob Hope Show armed with one-line zingers composed by their writers. Hope found great sport in jokes about Bing's loud shirts and weird color combinations (Bing was actually color-blind), his losing horses, his four sons, his money ("Bing doesn't actually file an income tax return; he just asks the government, 'How much do you need this year?' '').

Bing countered with cracks about Hope's cornball humor, his failed romances, his parsimony, his slight paunch. Bing claimed to have rendered Hope speechless on one memorable occasion. That was when Bing tossed the surprise line during a broadcast, "You know, Bob, from the rear you look like a sackful of cats being carried to the river."

Bing invited Bob to one of the entertainments staged the night before the Del Mar track opened.

"Supposing we do those old routines we did at the Capitol?" Bing suggested.

"Sure thing!" said the ever-eager Hope.

With his wife, Dixie Lee, at Santa Anita Park racetrack, Arcadia, California, 1945.

Bing, Philadelphia golf pro Jug McSpaden, bandleader Bob Crosby, and Bob Hope at a war bond exhibition golf tourney staged by

Bing and Bob at the Lakeside Golf Club, Los Angeles, 1944.

The show biz crowd was convulsed by the Hope-Crosby antics. One of those present was William LeBaron, production chief at Paramount. When he returned to the studio, he told his aides, "Those two boys worked well together. Let's find them a picture to do."

The studio had a dusty script that had once been fashioned for Burns and Allen. When they left Paramount, the story was converted into a vehicle to star Jack Oakie and Fred MacMurray. Oakie departed before the movie could be made. The new title was *The Road to Mandalay*.

"Mandalay doesn't sound sinister enough," said Don Hartman, who was converting the script for Crosby and Hope.

"How about making it *Road to Singapore?*" suggested his writing partner, Frank Butler.

Hope and Crosby never got to Singapore. Nor to Zanzibar, Morocco, Bali, or Utopia. The formula had them perennially on the Road seeking a fortune they never quite reached. Along the way they encountered cannibals, cops, other con men, villains of all stripes, and—Dorothy Lamour.

She was a New Orleans beauty who had combined a sultry contralto and a skimpy costume called a sarong into a rousing career as the heroine of South Seas adventures. She had appeared with Hope in *The Big Broadcast* but hadn't made a film with Crosby before *Road to Singapore*. She

A turbanned Bing and Bob in "Road to Morocco", 1942.

didn't know what she was getting into.

During the first scene with her two co-stars, Lamour watched in wonderment as the quips bounced back and forth.

"Hey, boys," she exclaimed, "will you please let me get my line in!"

It was like that. Both Bing and Bob handed the script to their radio writers and instructed them to supply gags. The two stars then tossed the lines into the scenes, much to the distaste of scenarists Hartman and Butler.

"Hey, Frank!" Hope yelled to Butler on the set one day. "If you hear anything that sounds like one of your lines, just shout 'Bingo!' "

The director, Victor Schertzinger, was delighted.

"I really shouldn't take money for this job," he told Hope and Crosby. "All I do is say 'stop' and 'go.' "

The combination of Hope and Crosby was magical. Bing played the charming schemer who got the pair in trouble, then managed to walk off with the girl. Hope was the eternal optimist, putting faith in his partner's plots, and hoping the girls would fall for him. They never did.

When *Road to Singapore* was released in 1940, it was a huge success, adding new luster to Crosby's career and establishing Hope as a box-office star. They and Lamour followed with *Road to Zanzibar* in 1941 and *Road to Morocco* in 1942. Later came *Utopia* (1946), *Rio* (1948), *Bali* (1953), and *Hong Kong* (1962). Crosby and Hope had been scheduled to make *Road to the Fountain of Youth* in 1978.

Few partners in show business history complemented each other so thoroughly.

Hope was a premier gagster who could sing. Crosby was a supreme singer who was clever with a quip. Hope had started his career as a dancer, and Crosby learned to hoof with a certain heavy-footed flair. But even beyond their superior talents, the relationship was right.

Although they could toss insults with the accuracy of a Bob Feller, there was no sting involved. The public believed that Bing and Bob were two men who really liked and enjoyed each other.

It was true. Bing admired Bob's energy

"Road to Singapore" (Paramount, 1940): Dorothy Lamour and Bing.

Dixie Lee Crosby and her four sons welcome Bing home, October 1941, from a South American trip. The sons (left to right), twins, Dennis and Philip, Lindsay, Gary and their mother met Bing in New York.

Gary Crosby, eldest of Bing's sons, makes his screen debut in "Star-Spangled Rhythm" 1943.

and ambition. Bob revered Bing's easygoing talent. They shared a love of golf and enjoyed all kinds of sports. Theirs was a deep and enduring respect for each other.

Bob learned early that friendship with Bing was not an easy thing to manage. Bing was subject to dark moods. At such times he would be absolutely unreachable, and those who tried received a cutting response.

Nor was Bing demonstrative. He disliked praise for himself and rarely gave it to others. He was ever wary of phonies, having known a great many in his early career. If Bing liked a person's company, he never said so. He expressed the feeling by *not* walking away.

Hope was entirely the opposite, a cheerful extrovert who totally enjoyed all the

A harmonious moment as Bing and a youthful Frank Sinatra sing in Crosby's dressing room in Hollywood, 1943.

"Road to Rio" (Paramount, 1948): The Weire Brothers.

honors that came to him. He was thrilled in 1950 when the Friars Club announced a big industry dinner saluting his achievements. A score of top stars would be there, including Bob's buddy from the Road pictures.

Bing never showed.

Hope didn't show his disappointment, but he was deeply hurt. When asked about his no-show, Bing replied, "My friendship for Bob doesn't depend on appearing at testimonials."

Golf and their movie and radio appearances put Bing and Bob together. Both lived in Toluca Lake, just over the hill from Hollywood, and they often played rounds together at the Lakeside Golf Club. Later Bing moved to Holmby Hills near the UCLA cam-

pus. Both were involved with their careers and families and saw little of each other outside of studios and golf tournaments.

Their closest time together came when they made *Road to Hong Kong* in England in 1961. Both stars took along their wives and children, and they rented a country manor called Cranbourne Court.

Hope recalled, "We had a ball. In the morning, Bing and I sailed off to the studio,

"Road to Hong Kong" (United Artists, 1962): Bing and Bob Hope on the road.

Dinah Shore and Bing entertain GIs in France, 1944.

only fourteen minutes away, in our chauffeured Rolls Royce. Our wives and children explored England while we toiled under the arc lamps. When the English crew broke for tea in the afternoon, Bing and I took a golf break. We could usually get in nine holes before darkness fell over the bogs.

"Then both families gathered in the dining room, which was big enough to hold a roller derby. Cranbourne Court came fully equipped with china, silver, and a full staff, including an Arthur Treacher-like butler who leaned toward the port. Every night the ham was glazed and so was the butler."

The war years brought Bing Crosby's greatest movie success.

Not only were the Road pictures immensely popular. Paramount was also producing a string of hits, including *Holiday*

Inn, which provided Bing's greatest song hit.

The idea for the movie was Irving Berlin's. Bing would play a successful man who tired of the rat race and decided to operate an inn that would be open only on holidays. He would be joined by Fred Astaire. The premise provided Berlin with an excuse to write a song about each of the major holidays.

What about Christmas? The New York songwriter got the idea while sitting in the sunshine of Beverly Hills. He brought the song to the studio and demonstrated it for Bing and the filmmakers. Berlin sang the new songs himself in his squeaky tenor, accompanying on a specially built piano that could shift keys with a lever.

All agreed that "White Christmas" was a catchy tune that would fit well in *Holiday Inn.* No one was prepared for the impact when the movie and Bing's Decca record were released. Bing himself never expected the result. He had recorded "White Christmas" in eighteen minutes.

In London, September 1944, Bing prepares to tour European military camps and bases.

Entertaining patients at the Philadelphia Naval Hospital, June 1945.

With World War II raging and millions of American young men away from home, the wistful remembrance of an oldtime Christmas struck everyone.

"So many young people were away and they'd hear the song at that time of year and it would really affect them. I sang it many times in the field in Europe for the soldiers. They'd holler for it, they'd demand it, and

I'd sing it and they'd all cry. It was really sad."

There were no dry eyes at the Hollywood Canteen one Christmas Eve after Bing appeared at the back door with his four sons. They went onstage and sang "White Christmas" to a packed house.

Bing disliked playing benefits, preferring to do his charitable work in a quieter manner. But he gave his talents liberally to the war effort, making tours that sold $14 million worth of war bonds. He organized Crosby Camp Tours and traveled 50,000 miles entertaining the troops. He remarked later that his tours through wartime England, France, and Germany were "the most satisfying and rewarding experience in my career."

Bing crossed the Atlantic on the *Ile de France*, sleeping in a tiny cubicle near quarters for the paratroopers. In England he made recordings with Glenn Miller's Air Force band and broadcast to the German people, who knew him as Der Bingle. He visited General Eisenhower's headquarters at Versailles. The Commander in Chief of the Allied Forces joined with Bing and two officers in a barbershop quartet.

"Is there anything I can do for you?" Crosby asked.

"Yes, you might send me some hominy grits," said Eisenhower. "I can't get any over here."

Crosby mentioned the request at a press conference on his return to the United States. Later he received a cable from Eisenhower. "Call off the grits. I've got grits spilling all over this area."

Going My Way sprang from the inventive mind of an erratic, irreverent Irishman named Leo McCarey.

He had been a gag writer and director for Laurel and Hardy shorts. He also directed Harold Lloyd in *The Milky Way* and Cary Grant and Irene Dunne in *The Awful Truth*.

McCarey had the Irish fondness for the malt, as did his brother Ray, who was also a film director. Ray never achieved the level of his brother's success, and their mother once pointed out the reason. "Leo drinks between making pictures and Ray makes pictures between drinks."

Leo also enjoyed betting on the nags, and he became acquainted with Bing Crosby at the race tracks.

"Bing, I'm working on a script I want you to do," Leo said one day.

"Yeah? What's it called?" Bing asked.

"*Padre*."

"*Padre*, huh? I don't think I could play a Mexican father."

"No, I want you to play a priest."

Bing laughed. "Are you kidding? Me, a busker, a strolling minstrel? Why, I'd be excommunicated if I tried."

"I don't think so. I think you'd be one helluva priest."

Bing refused to entertain the notion, but McCarey persisted. One day the director related his story to Bing. It was about a young priest whose modern ideas allowed him to relate to youngsters in the parish, and an older priest with firm ties to tradition and Ireland.

When McCarey finished, Bing was in tears, a rare occurrence for him.

"Okay, Leo, I'll do it," Bing said.

Bing was king of Paramount, and the studio agreed to sponsor McCarey's project, which he now called *Going My Way*. There were misgivings, however. McCarey talked a good picture, but there was little script to show. Furthermore, McCarey's work habits did not conform to studio standards.

Paramount's fears seemed to be confirmed. Bing, Barry Fitzgerald, who played the older priest, Rise Stevens, and other members of the cast reported each morning only to find McCarey tinkling a piano, searching for a fugitive melody. That might continue into the afternoon until Leo came up with an idea for the next scene. The

Marjorie Reynolds, Fred Astaire, and a quizzical Bing in "Holiday Inn" (Paramount, 1942).

shooting schedule stretched to six months, and even Bing wondered if he had been right in accepting the movie.

Going My Way was the biggest hit of 1944 and it won Oscars as best picture, for Leo McCarey's direction, with script by Frank Butler and Frank Cavett, Barry Fitzgerald as

supporting actor, Johnny Burke and James Van Heusen for the song "Swinging on a Star" and—Bing Crosby, best performance by an actor.

Bing almost didn't make the ceremonies at Grauman's Chinese Theater. Paramount officials located him on the golf course and

Fred Astaire and Bing ham it up during a USO
tour in France, 1944.

Bing examines an invention offered by his
research foundation in Pasadena, California,
during World War II.

Bing and Bob Hope enter-
tain veteran Harold Russell on
the movie set of "Road to Rio", 1947.

Bing hams it up in a studio commissary.

Dinah Shore and Bing entertain the American Third Army in France for the USO, 1944.

During a visit to the Metropolitan Opera House in New York in December 1945, Bing accompanies Patrice Munsel on a piano in her dressing room. Munsel played Juliet in Romeo and Juliet.

"Going My Way" (Paramount, 1944): Oscar winners Bing and Barry Fitzgerald.

urged him to attend. He did so with reluctance.

Gary Cooper made the announcement. "The winner is . . . Bing Crosby for *Going My Way*."

Crosby walked to the stage, incredulous.

"This is the only country," he told the audience, "where an old broken-down crooner can win an Oscar for acting. It shows that everybody in this country has a chance to succeed. I was just lucky to have Leo McCarey take me by the hand and lead me through the picture."

McCarey and Crosby were already at work on a sequel, *The Bells of St. Mary's*. Bing was repeating his role as Father O'Malley, with Ingrid Bergman playing the feisty nun, Sister Benedict. On the same night that Bing had won his Oscar, Bergman received her award for her performance in *Gaslight*. On the morning after

Father O'Malley doffs his priestly robes, for a scene in "Going My Way", 1944.

Bing, honored for his performance in "Going My Way", and Ingrid Bergman, recognized for her role in "Gaslight", compare Oscars in Los Angeles, 1945.

the awards, *The Bells of St. Mary's* set was the scene of fervent celebration.

Bing found the Swedish star a delight. Together with the impish McCarey, they played a devilish trick on the movie's technical adviser, a serious-minded priest named Father Devlin.

The best film performers of 1944 were honored at an Academy Award function in Hollywood in March 1945. Oscars went to (left to right) Barry Fitzgerald for best supporting actor in "Going My Way", Ingrid Bergman for best actress in "Gaslight", and Bing Crosby for best actor in "Going My Way".

The Catholic hierarchy was understandably nervous about *The Bells of St. Mary's,* since it costarred one of the screen's great beauties and a most attractive actor as nun and priest working together. Father Devlin was on the set every day, watching closely lest the relationship between Bergman and Crosby lapse into sensuality.

One day McCarey rehearsed a scene between the two stars, taking place in Father O'Malley's office. "Okay, let's shoot it," said the director, and the cameras rolled.

Father O'Malley and Sister Benedict discussed St. Mary's business, then his hand brushed hers. They gazed soulfully into each other's eyes, then he slipped his arm around her. Their lips met in a passionate kiss that lasted until McCarey called "Cut!"

Father Devlin stared in open-mouthed horror. He was about to speak when McCarey, Crosby, Bergman, and the entire crew exploded in laughter. The scene had been staged for the technical adviser's benefit.

"You've just removed five years from my life," said Father Devlin.

A serious exchange between Ingrid Bergman and Bing in "The Bells of St. Mary's", 1945.

Bing at the Top

Bing Crosby at war's end was clearly the reigning star of the entertainment world.

Besides the Oscar, he had won every honor in the film industry and remained the Number 1 box-office draw. His records outsold those of every other singer, including sensational newcomers like Frank Sinatra and Dick Haymes. The Kraft Music Hall continued among the top-ranked radio programs in audience ratings, setting the standard for literacy and style.

Bing was a total professional, but he insisted on doing things his way. He abhorred routine, and for that reason he came into conflict with his longtime radio sponsor, Kraft, and his network, NBC. Predictably, Bing won out in the dispute, in the meantime bringing a revolution to the broadcast industry.

"I want to record my radio show," he announced.

The news caused an earthquake on Madison Avenue and in the executive suites of Rockefeller Plaza. It was heresy. Since the beginning of network radio, everything went out live. Not only were all the major programs heard instantly as they were performed; they also had to be presented twice, for the Eastern and Western time zones.

"It's a waste of time," Bing argued. "It also makes for slipshod entertainment. If I could put forty-five minutes on record, then cut out the dull spots and the failed jokes, it'd be a much better half-hour show."

Bing had a personal reason for the proposal, too. He hated the routine of reporting to Sunset and Vine every Thursday, thirty-nine weeks a year, then trying to maintain spontaneity during two complete broadcasts. By recording several programs at a time, he would be free to travel to golf tournaments, to go fishing with his sons, and to hunt with friends like Clark Gable and Gary Cooper.

Bing returns to Hollywood in December 1943, sporting a beard which he grew while on vacation at his Nevada ranch.

**At the Stork Club in New York City
with his wife Dixie Lee, 1943.**

"Absolutely not!" NBC thundered.

"Never!" Kraft agreed.

"Okay, then," Bing replied, "get yourself another boy." He took a walk from the Kraft Music Hall.

Law suits and threats of blacklisting followed. Bing held his ground. Philco agreed to sponsor him on a recorded show, and Bing took it to the American Broadcasting Company, then a poor third among the nation's networks.

"The Bing Crosby Show" made its debut on October 16, 1946, over ABC. Bing had tired of the blasé audiences in Hollywood radio studios, and he took the show to San Francisco for the first broadcast. It was not a total success.

"Mr. Crosby has delivered a major, if not fatal, blow to the outworn and unrealistic prejudice against the recorded program," said the *New York Times*. But critics and listeners had misgivings about the quality of the broadcasts. The Crosby voice was not coming through loud and clear, as it had in American living rooms for more than a decade.

"The Bing Crosby Show" began to drop in the ratings.

"We told you so!" trumpeted the moguls of NBC and CBS.

"I had confidence that a recorded show

would be just as satisfactory entertainment-wise as a live show, better in many ways. But everybody was against the idea—the networks, the sponsors, the agencies. They thought it might hurt the networks financially. They felt if entertainers were allowed to record, they could sell to individual stations instead of having to use the networks. The way it worked out, it didn't seem to hurt the networks."

Bing would not be defeated. Earlier he had formed Bing Crosby Enterprises to develop new products. One of the engineers was John Mullin, who had marveled at the quality of German broadcasts during the war. He discovered that the Germans had developed a technique of recording on tape, thus eliminating the surface noise of records.

Mullin managed to bring home a pair of German tape machines, and he perfected them at Bing Crosby Enterprises. Bing's radio show was presented on tape for the first time on October 1, 1947, and the result was extraordinary. Crosby Enterprises combined with the Ampex Company to merchandise the tape machines.

The other networks and the ad agencies caved in. Every radio star wanted taped shows, and live primetime programs virtually vanished, except for sports and news. Eventually videotape became standard in the television industry.

Bing visits Ingrid Bergman on the set of "Arch of Triumph", her twelfth role in US pictures, 1946.

A happy time for Bing and friends on a
fishing trip in Sun Valley, Idaho, 1945.

Fishing with friends at Maligne Lake,
Jasper National Park, Alberta, Canada,
1946.

It's a bunt for Bing during a softball game at Jasper National Park, Alberta, Canada, 1946.

Onlookers watch intently as Bing blasts his way out of a sand trap at the National Celebrities Golf Tourney in May 1947.

Under Everett Crosby's watchful eye, Bing's investments were being pushed into other areas also. Bing was advised during a golf game with Jock Whitney to invest in a frozen juice company—Minute Maid; it became a huge moneymaker. Along with Bob Hope, Bing made some prudent investments in oil exploration. Bing Crosby Enterprises produced his radio shows and some of his movies, and later moved into television with series such as "Fireside Theater" and "Ben Casey." Bing bought an 18,000-

Crosby relaxes with Coleen Gray on the set of "Riding High" after filming in a muddy stable, Hollywood, 1949.

On the set of "Top o' the Morning" (Paramount, 1949).

acre ranch at Elko, Nevada, where his sons spent summers helping to herd the 4,500 head of cattle. Bings Things, Inc., marketed gadgets.

Although Everett supervised the business interests, Bing took part in all major decisions. He was meticulous about his correspondence and carried a portable Dictaphone wherever he went. Bing's letters were often warm and humorous, in contrast to his demeanor in person.

To his associates and those of us who interviewed him, the real Bing Crosby contrasted starkly with the easygoing image he projected over radio and on the screen.

Bing was a classic loner. Many who believed that they had a lock on his friend-

Bing visits Judy Garland on the set of Metro-Goldwyn-Mayer's "The Harvey Girls" 1945.

ship discovered to their sorrow that it was not possible. If Bing thought he was being used or someone was pushing too hard, that person was suddenly dropped from Bing's acquaintance.

He had absolutely no tolerance for boredom. When he lost interest in a conversation, which was usually after the first few sentences, he merely walked away. He was the master of the see-through stare. You might have thought he was looking at you, but his gaze went through and beyond, as if you were a pane of glass. When boredom set in, his blue eyes glazed over.

Bing could be unpredictable. He could walk down Vine Street from the Brown

Danny Kaye (right) entertains Bing and director George Seaton on the set of the film "White Christmas", Hollywood, 1947.

Derby to the NBC studios completely oblivious to fans asking for autographs or hangers-on seeking favors. Then he might suddenly focus attention on a parking lot attendant and discuss whether the Yankees would win the pennant again.

When Bing finished a radio rehearsal once, he was accosted by a former soldier who wanted Bing to hear his singing voice. Bing agreed and went back to the studio to listen to the boy sing.

"You sing pretty good," Bing agreed, and he volunteered some pointers, adding, "The best way to get started is to get a job with a bandleader."

"But how do I get in to see one?" the hopeful asked.

"How did you get in here?" Bing replied, walking away.

Bing would not be pushed into anything. The Crosbys were stalwart Republicans, and in 1940 Larry Crosby announced that Bing

Taking off from his set for "Top o' the Morning", Bing tries out his Christmas present, a new camera, as Angela Lansbury looks on, 1948.

was endorsing Thomas Dewey over Franklin Roosevelt. Reporters were surprised, because Bing had never before committed himself to a candidate. Reporters reached him on a hunting trip and asked if he was taking part in the campaign.

"Who's running?" said Bing.

Interviewing Bing was hazardous. Columnist Army Archerd recalled the occasion when he tried to get some answers from Bing on the Paramount lot. Bing mounted his bicycle in mid-question, and Archerd ran alongside as he penned the replies.

I once asked Bing if he had any theory about publicity.

"Naw, I'm just too lazy to worry about it."

Was Bing lazy? Bob Hope claimed he was.

"I'll tell you how lazy Bing is. If he made his own movie, he'd open up with himself peering through the knothole of a fence. The rest of the picture would be what he saw."

Although Bing's professional acquaintance was wide, he had few close friends. Mostly they were amusing characters who

didn't make demands on him—his gag writer, Barney Dean; the producer of his radio show, Bill Morrow; songwriter Johnny Burke.

Once Bing and a gag man spent a weekend at Bing's summer home at Del Mar. Bing laughed and sang and in one surprising moment said to his companion, "I like you." Then he added, "I like you because you don't ask me any questions."

Bing was rarely given to introspection, in public or in private. In his last years he

A light-hearted moment for Bing, Bob Crosby, and Ann Blyth during production of "Top o' the Morning", Hollywood, 1948.

allowed a modicum of self-analysis.

"I'm not very effusive. I'm not very demonstrative. I just never have been. My mother was the same way; my father was just the opposite. I don't know why, it's just something I've inherited. I may think a lot of a person, but I seldom tell them so. I'll tell them about their ability.... I've never told a friend that 'I love you' or 'I like you' and if any friend told me that, I'd be very embarrassed and I wouldn't know what to do.... What it boils down to is that I'm very undemonstrative and that problem has given rise to the belief that I'm a loner and I live behind an 'ice curtain.' "

Some of Bing's friends believed that his withdrawal was caused in large part by his troubles with Dixie.

Theirs was an almost invisible Hollywood marriage, since Dixie was rarely seen in public. They had their quarrels over his aloofness, his neglect of their sons, his many absences for hunting, fishing, golf. It was common Hollywood knowledge that Dixie drank.

In 1950, Larry Crosby admitted that his brother and Dixie had had a serious quarrel. "If they take this to court, I hope it will be a

John Derek looks on as Anne Baxter presents the Golden Apple Award to Bing, dressed as Santa Claus at the Holly-wood Women's Press Club's Christmas Party. William Holden stands by.

Gary Cooper, Clark Gable, and Bing.

Bing sits on Groucho Marx's knee during a comedy routine for the film "Mr. Music" in Hollywood, 1950.

legal separation, not a divorce. The family would want it that way. My brother's a Catholic, Dixie is not."

Again Bing put down his brother.

"As far as I know there's nothing to it," Bing said in Paris. "Some columnist must have started it."

In 1952, Dixie's fragile health began to fail. She underwent an abdominal operation in July, but it was too late to stop the cancer. She died on November 1, 1952. The loss hit Bing harder than his friends had expected it would. When he talked about Dixie in later years, he remembered only the good times.

"She was a very fine woman. I was devoted to her. She was very timid, terribly shy. It was awfully difficult to get her to make any kind of public appearance, and that was the reason she never did anything more in show business. She just hated the exposure and the necessity to work with strangers. When she did get to know anybody, she was a marvelous friend and a great deal of fun. . . . She was interested in

Son Lindsay gets a golf lesson during a vacation at the Trianon Palace Hotel, Versailles, France, 1953.

At a benefit softball game at Coeur D'Alene, Idaho, 1949, Bing and his sons (left to right) Philip, Lindsay, Gary, and Dennis are ready for play.

Bing and his first family at their home in Beverly Hills, June 1952. Front row: Bing and Lindsay. Back row: Twins Dennis and Philip, Dixie Lee Crosby, and Gary.

Bing and son Lindsay.

Bing, head bowed and arm around his son, Lindsay, after a mass for his wife, Dixie Lee, in Beverly Hills, November 1952.

Bing looks over his birthday cake while Dorothy Lamour and Bob Hope enjoy the **surprise party given during the filming of "Road to Bali", 1952.**

everything the children did, was very severe with them, and they all loved her very much."

Bing was concerned about his own performance as a father and in a widely quoted interview claimed he had failed his sons.

"I think I failed them by giving them too much work and discipline, too much money, and too little time and attention," Bing said. "I just want them to be nice guys. I don't care how big they are or how important. I'd just like them to be the kind that other people would like to have around. And I want them to be thoughtful of other people. I hate thoughtlessness, rudeness, and arrogance."

None of the Crosby boys finished college and at one time all four were married to Las Vegas showgirls. Not unlike their father, the sons engaged in some drunken escapades that hit the papers.

Gary recorded a hit tune with his father, "Sam's Song," and launched a promising career as a singer and actor. All four Crosbys joined in a nightclub act that played Las Vegas and other cities. The reviews were poor and the quartet broke up.

The Crosby sons denied their father's claim of failure.

"Dad was always there when we needed him," said Philip.

"I don't know of many fathers who gave more consideration to their children," added Lindsay. "Certainly he had to be away a good deal of the time. But what about all those summers we spent together? Two months on the ranch at Elko, another month at Hayden Lake in Idaho. And after Mom died, he took me to Europe for nine months. I can't understand how he can say now that he didn't give us enough of his time."

The public statements did not help the relationship between father and sons. The gap widened when Bing took a bride younger than Gary and began raising a second family.

But then, Dennis pointed out, "Dad told us many times that he was responsible for us only till we were twenty-one."

After seeing the boys' act for the first time, Bing poses with his four sons, Philip (left), Lindsay, Gary (rear), and Dennis, **backstage at the Moulin Rouge in Hollywood, 1959.**

A Legend in His Time

By the mid-1950s, Bing Crosby was beginning to slow the pace he had maintained in his career for a quarter-century. He was well into middle age and past the time he could play the serenading romantic in film musicals. In 1954 he acted his most dramatic role as the alcoholic stage star in *The Country Girl* with Grace Kelly and William Holden. Bing had his third Academy Award nomination for the film (his second had been for *The Bells of St. Mary's*), and Miss Kelly won the Oscar for best actress.

Kelly and Crosby costarred again in M-G-M's *High Society*, a remake of *The Philadelphia Story*, with Frank Sinatra, Celeste Holm and a splendid Cole Porter score. In 1957, Bing again played an alcoholic in *Man on Fire*, the first movie in which he did not sing.

With his Paramount contract ended after twenty-four years, Bing's movies became

Wife Kathryn and Bing prepare to take their eight-day-old son Harry Lillis Crosby, Jr., home from a Los Angeles hospital, 1958.

less frequent—only seven in the last twenty years of his life.

The Bing Crosby radio show, like all other major radio programs, died of malnutrition of sponsorship. All the big advertising money was pouring into television, but Bing was in no hurry to join the new medium. He had made his TV debut in 1952 with fellow sportsman Hope in a telethon to raise funds for American athletes to attend the Olympic Games.

When his radio show ended in 1955, Bing bided his time.

"Anybody who allows himself to appear on television once a week is out of his mind," he commented. "Exposure like that devours you."

When Crosby finally made his debut as a TV star in 1955, he did so with a splashy revue costarring Frank Sinatra, Rosemary Clooney, and son Lindsay. The show was a success, and Bing followed with a musical version of Maxwell Anderson's fantasy, *High Tor*, with a young costar fresh from Britain, Julie Andrews. Having turned fifty, he began dropping hints that he might withdraw from show business.

"I suppose I really should retire," he told me in an interview. "People are going to start saying, 'Why the hell doesn't he quit?'"

But he explained why he couldn't retire completely. "I have some hefty commitments to charity every year. As long as I'm working, I can donate up to thirty per cent of my salaries. If I didn't work, I would have to take the money out of principal, and that's not a good idea."

In response to a query from the music column of the London *Daily Express*, Bing wrote that he was "long gone."

He explained, "I just don't sing as well as I used to. I'm not as enthusiastic as I used to be, the feel for a song isn't there, the desire to sing, to be in action—and when this is ab-

French actress Martine Carrol and Bing join talents along Paris's Champs Élysées in May 1953 to sell tickets for an annual charity ba- **zaar. The proceeds went to the 2nd Armored Division Veterans of France.**

Grace Kelly aims her camera at Bing on the set of "The Country Girl".

Costars Bing and Donald O'Connor on the set of Paramount's "Anything Goes" 1955.

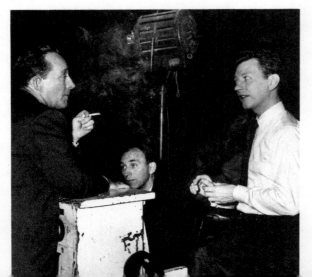

sent, so is the style."

Bing was unsettled in his personal life. All the boys had left home, and he felt alone in the big Holmby Hills house. After the shock of Dixie's passing had gone, he started quietly dating, usually with young actresses such as Mona Freeman, Rhonda Fleming, or Mary Murphy. There was also a starlet from Columbia Pictures named Kathryn Grant.

She had been born Olive Grandstaff in West Columbia, Texas. She was a beauty queen at the Houston Fat Stock Show, where Roy Rogers recommended a Hollywood career. She landed at Paramount at the age of eighteen, and that's where she met Bing. They dated after she moved to

Columbia Pictures, and she was converted to Bing's faith.

In September 1956, reporters were alerted that Bing was going to marry young Miss Grant at his Hayden Lake place. He had applied to the Tacoma parish for his baptismal record, a requirement in the Catholic church for marriage; she had bought a wedding dress.

"When will the wedding be, Bing?" a newsman asked.

"What wedding?" he replied.

There was none. The distraught Kathryn returned to the studio, and her boss, Harry Cohn, sympathetically put her to work on movies and publicity tours. She didn't talk to Bing for a year.

In October 1957, the telephone rang in Kathryn's apartment.

"This is Bing!"

"Yes?"

"Kathryn, what I have to say to you will take only about a minute."

"Good. That's about all the time I have. I'm on my way to church."

"Let's get married."

The wedding took place at St. Anne's Church in Las Vegas on October 24, 1957. The bride, twenty-three, wore a white suit with purple orchid and lace mantilla. The bridegroom, fifty-three, was dressed in a blue pinstripe suit with white shirt and blue tie.

"Mrs. Crosby! How about that!" Bing exclaimed as he left the church.

Bing had tired of the Hollywood life, and he and his bride moved 400 miles north to Hillsborough, on the San Francisco peninsula. Three children arrived within four years—Harry Lillis, Jr., August 8, 1958; Mary Frances (at last, a daughter!), September 14, 1959; Nathaniel Patrick, October 29, 1961.

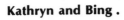

Kathryn and Bing .

Newlyweds Bing and Kathryn on their honeymoon in Palm Springs, October 1957.

Bing, Kathryn, and daughter Mary Frances, 4, sing "Happy Birthday" as son Nathaniel blows out the candles for his third birthday, 1964.

Gary Crosby and his father sport similar outfits for a segment of Bing's television show in Hollywood, September 1964.

"Perhaps I was too strict with my four sons. Certainly I didn't emphasize the right sense of values. I thought I did, but none of them ever finished college. With my new kids I'm going to emphasize the importance of art and music and the literary classics and sort of de-emphasize athletics and see what comes out. Love is the important thing: love and the right sense of values, which include a respect for people, a love of God, and a pride in achievement."

Bing had twenty good years with his new family. He was continually amazed and delighted with the energy of his young wife, who struggled through five years of study to become a registered nurse.

"I bet her a piece of jewelry that she would

Kathryn, Bing, and their three children, Nathaniel, 2; Mary Frances, 4; and Harry, Jr., 5, at the Sports and Boat Show in San Francisco, 1964.

Bing and Inger Stevens stand before the
camera while the film crew lines up mike
and lights for the next scene of Man on
Fire, 1957.

With Inger Stevens, Bing takes a break
during the filming of Man on Fire, 1957.

**Being made up for the film "High Time"
with Nicole Maurey, 1960.**

In London, 1975, Bing with wife Kathryn and Bob Hope.

never pass the state boards," said the proud husband. "Well, she came out first in the Los Angeles area and fourth in the state of California. She made a chump of me."

For a man who kept talking about retirement, Bing kept surprisingly busy. He made his last movie, a remake of *Stagecoach*, in 1966, and he continued with a couple of TV specials a year, guest appearances with Hope and others, and occasional record dates. He and the family spent much time at Las Cruces

and Mazátlan in Mexico, where Bing enjoyed the fishing and golf.

An interviewer once asked Bing what he would change if he had it to do all over again.

"I wouldn't change a thing," he replied. "I would do it just exactly the same way—by singing. I had a wonderful time. I would want everything to be the same."

With a bit of prodding from Kathryn, Bing began reactivating his singing career in

1976. He sang a few concerts in the San Francisco area, then played the London Palladium to great acclaim. In October, he appeared at the Los Angeles Music Center, marking the first time he had sung publicly in Los Angeles since the Cocoanut Grove days. His wife and their three children came on stage for some songs and patter.

The reason for the concerts was to help charities, he explained, but also to give his kids a chance to perform.

"This new family gets very little opportunity to work or to appear. They do a Christmas TV show, then go back to school or back to golf. So they're not very expert or polished performers. Mary Frances is a very good dancer; Harry can play piano, guitar, sing; Nathaniel can do dialogue or whatever you want. They can rehearse and prac-

Bing watches wife Kathryn practice her golf swing at their Hillsborough home near San Francisco, December 1975.

Bing and Pearl Bailey enjoy rehearsal for a TV special, 1974.

tice, but they can't get anywhere unless they work in front of an audience."

Bing had returned to concerts, despite a serious operation in early 1974. A lung ailment had been diagnosed as pneumonia, but he didn't respond to treatment. Cancer was feared, and two-fifths of his left lung was removed. The trouble had been caused by a rare fungus he had contracted during an African safari.

On March 3, 1977, Bing was taping a CBS television special saluting his fifty years in show business. Toward the end of the program in Pasadena's Ambassador Auditorium, the audience was horrified when Bing fell off the stage and into the orchestra pit. A ruptured disc kept him bedridden for months.

Still, he came back.

In September, he and his family were in London for the taping of his annual Christmas television show. Then they appeared at the Palladium for a two-week sellout engagement. Afterward, Kathryn and the children returned to the United States, while Bing decided to play some golf in Spain.

He had finished a round at Madrid's La Moraleja with three Spanish champions when he fell dead.

The American ambassador telephoned Kathryn the news. Red-eyed but brave, she appeared before reporters at her Hillsborough home.

"I can't think of any better way for a golfer who sings for a living to finish the round," she said, fighting back tears.

"He's always been a very simple man. I think he is remembered in songs, isn't he? I think that's the way it should be."

At New York's Aqueduct Race Track, April 1976, Bing checks over the racing form.

Former President Ford chats with Bing and Kathryn at the Crosby Pro-Am golf tourney in Pebble Beach, California, January 1977.

Like a seasoned resident of the Big Apple, Bing takes the subway for a day at New York's Aqueduct race track, April 1976.

On a tour of Athens with his family in July 1969, Bing visits the Acropolis.

Following surgery to remove a nonmalignant lung growth, Crosby relaxes in Las Cruces, Mexico, in April 1974.

Bing and Kathryn with a billboard advertising their show at the London Palladium in England, September 1977.

Bing, recovered from damage to a spinal disc, leaves the hospital with Kathryn, in April 1977. He was injured when he toppled into an orchestra pit while taping a television show.

Bob Hope was in New York, scheduled for a benefit that night in Morristown, New Jersey. For the first time in his career, he canceled.

"I just can't get funny tonight," he told me.

President Carter issued the statement: "For all the roads he traveled in his memorable career, Bing Crosby remained a gentleman, proof that a great talent can be a good man despite the pressures of show business. He lived a life his fans around the

In a scene from their 1976 Christmas television special, Bing, Kathryn, and their three children, Nathaniel (left), Harry Lillis, Jr., and Mary Frances.

Bing and Cesar de Zulueta at the "19th Hole" bar of La Moraleja golf club just before Bing's last golf game, October 14, 1977.

world felt was typically American: successful yet modest; casual but elegant."

Crosby's death from a massive heart attack caused an outpouring of sorrow and a wealth of editorial comment.

The *New York Times* said, "Young Americans are used to pop stars who are angry, sexy and rebellious. Bing Crosby answered different needs for a different age. He did so with a grace that was typical of his whole career, and in his own subtle and unassuming way, he left a mark on American popular music that many more flashy performers would find hard to match."

Harry Crosby, Jr., who was nineteen, now had to assume his new position as head man of the family. He flew to Madrid and made the necessary arrangements. Harry and the family butler, Alan Fisher, made the mournful journey back to California with the crucifix-topped casket—and with Bing's golf clubs. The widow and her two other children, Mary Frances, eighteen, and Nathaniel, fifteen, met the flight in Los Angeles.

Bing had specified that he wanted a quiet, private funeral. That was accomplished

Bing swings at the 1st hole at La Moraleja golf club near Madrid, Spain, October 14, 1977. Only a short time later he collapsed on the course as the result of a heart attack.

Kathryn talks with newsmen in Los Angeles, October 1977, shortly after the arrival of her husband's casket from Spain.

Comedian Bob Hope and his wife, Delores, arrive for the early morning funeral services for Bing in Los Angeles.

Kathryn and her son Harry arrive for funeral services for her husband in Los Angeles, October 1977.

Mary Frances and Nathaniel Crosby, Bing's youngest children, arrive for their father's funeral.

by scheduling it at 6 A.M. the following morning.

Not a single fan appeared on the quiet side street near the UCLA campus where St. Paul's Church was located. The press was there in the predawn chill to record the arrivals of the thirty-five family members and longtime friends and associates. Kathryn Crosby arrived early with her three children, her head high. There was Rosemary Clooney, who had sung with Bing in his last concerts. Phil Harris, his old golf and hunting buddy. Bob Crosby, who spent his lifetime in the shadow of his famous brother. Bing's and Dixie's four sons—Gary, Dennis, Philip, and Lindsay. Bing's sister, Mary Rose Pool, and Kathryn's sister, Frances Meyer. Also Bing's lawyer, his secretary, his producer, and a scattering of friends.

Bob Hope was the last to arrive, accompanied by Dolores. He seemed somber, shaken.

The mourners filed into the tiny chapel. Bing lay in an oak casket between the two rows of choir chairs. Atop the casket was a blanket of red roses, the only flowers in the chapel. The casket was open, and Bing's face seemed calm and serene.

Father Elwood Kieser, who had known Bing when he lived in nearby Holmby Hills and had converted Kathryn to Catholicism, recited the Mass of the Resurrection. The simple service was the way Bing had wanted it, the priest said.

"Bing could laugh because he knew how to cry," he added. "He knew how to cry because he believed so fully in the Lord."

Kathryn Crosby emerged from the chapel and faced the lights of the television cameras. She was followed by her daughter and Bing's six sons, who were to lower his casket into the earth of Holy Cross Cemetery, near the graves of Bing's parents and Dixie.

As the mourners traveled through the still dark Los Angeles streets to the cemetery, their minds were filled with memories of Bing—memories that had been stirred by the soft notes of the chapel organ playing songs he had sung so well. "Blue Skies," "The Bells of St. Mary's," "Wait Till the Sun Shines, Nellie," "Wrap Your Troubles in Dreams," "Galway Bay," and

Too–ra loo–ra loo–ral,
too–ra loo–ra lie,
too–ra loo–ra loo–ral,
That's an Irish lullaby. [1]

A flash of the inimitable Crosby grin during rehearsal for a 1974 TV special.

The One and Only Bing 91

An Illustrated Filmography

by Norm Goldstein

Introduction

Bing Crosby was first, foremost, and forever a singer. The Crooner. The Groaner. Der Bingle. Word images that refer to his mellow, easy-going singing style.

But it is for just those qualities—his voice, his relaxed and warm presence—that we affectionately remember Bing Crosby as a movie actor, as well.

From the well-known series of Road pictures he made with Bob Hope and Dorothy Lamour (seven in all, and planning yet another when he died) to his Academy Award-winning portrayal in *Going My Way* and to his dramatic roles (such as in *The Country Girl*), Bing Crosby's very special qualities made him a leading and lasting performer through some thirty-five years and more than sixty films.

Mack Sennett caught the Crosby singing

With Bob Hope in a duet from "Variety Girl" Paramount 1947.

act at the Cocoanut Grove nightclub in Los Angeles and immediately felt that Bing's unusual combination of voice and personality would find an identifying response in audiences. He signed Crosby to a series of two-reelers in 1930, just as the film industry was beginning to learn how to deal with that new phenomenon—the talkies.

"The principal secret of Bing's success," Sennett has said, "is his ability to relax."

"What struck me about this guy was that all the stuffed shirts at the Grove stopped dancing and gathered around the bandstand to watch him croon. They came to hear him night after night. He held 'em."

In the Sennett shorts, in which he played with such female leads of the time as Babe Kane, Bing sang "I Surrender, Dear," "Blue of the Night," and "Just One More Chance."

Crosby's first real feature film, however, was *King of Jazz* in 1930. The "King of Jazz" in those Depression days was Paul Whiteman. Crosby had been singing with the band as part of a trio with Al Rinker and

Harry Barris—"The Rhythm Boys."

In *King of Jazz*, Crosby sang "Music Has Charms" over the credits, and the singing team had four specialties, including "So the Bluebirds and Blackbirds Got Together."

With the help of brother Everett, who took over as Bing's manager, the young Crosby got a couple of unbilled singing scenes in 1931 movies—a Douglas Fairbanks starrer, *Reaching for the Moon*, and *Confessions of a Coed*" (he got $500 for the latter).

It was then that Bing signed his CBS Radio contract and also appeared successfully at the Paramount Theater in New York. Armed with those plaudits, he signed a contract with Paramount Pictures, beginning with *The Big Broadcast* in 1932.

The reviews of the singer's first Paramount films foretold the things to come: "Crosby hints at great possibilities as a film player. No radio star ever has photographed better, or faced the cameras with greater poise and assurance than the pleasing Bing."

Those first movies were *College Humor* (1933—singing drama professor); *Too Much Harmony* (1933—musical comedy star); *Going Hollywood* (1933—a radio crooner); *We're Not Dressing* (1934—singing deck hand); and *She Loves Me Not* (1934—an undergraduate Princetonian).

By the beginning of 1934, Crosby was one of the screen's ten leading box office stars, along with Mae West, Wallace Beery, and Marie Dressler, among others.

He did the screen version of the Howard Lindsay-Russel Crouse musical comedy, *Anything Goes* (1936), in which he and Charlie Ruggles played the roles originated by William Gaxton and Victor Moore. Most of the memorable tunes were written by Cole Porter.

Then came *Rhythm on the Range* (1936). That film marked Martha Raye's film debut and Bing sang "I'm an Old Cowhand."

Other important films for Crosby in that period were *Two for Tonight* (1935); *Missis-*

Mischa Auer and Bing in "East Side of Heaven", 1939.

"Sing You Sinners" (Paramount, 1938): The singers are Bing, Fred MacMurray, and a very young Donald O'Connor.

sippi (1935); *Pennies From Heaven* (1936—the title song became a classic); *Waikiki Wedding* (1937—the hit song was "Sweet Leilani"); *Sing You Sinners* (1938); and *Paris Honeymoon* (1939).

It was in *Sing You Sinners* that Crosby really found the casual acting mode his audiences loved. Primarily a dramatic film, it costarred Fred MacMurray and Donald O'Connor as Crosby's younger brothers. The highlight of the movie was Bing's rendi-

tion of "Small Fry."

It was in 1940 that Bing began the movie road that led him to a series of memorable, everlasting enjoyments. He costarred in *Road to Singapore* with Bob Hope. It was the first of the enormously successful *Road* pictures, lightweight ventures in which the pair were usually two footloose travelers in an exotic land, where they promptly ran into trouble with a beautiful girl, Dorothy Lamour.

"Road to Zanzibar" (Paramount, 1941): Bob Hope and Bing are surrounded.

Perhaps the best of the "Road" pictures was *Road to Zanzibar*, a Tarzan-jungle spoof made in 1941. The others were: *Road to Morocco* (1942); *Road to Utopia* (1946); *Road to Rio* (1948); *Road to Bali* (1953—the first Road picture done in color); and *Road to Hong Kong* (1962).

In later years, Crosby was to tell an interviewer:

Bing and Bob Hope scale new heights in "Road to Utopia" 1946.

"The Road pictures were fun to do, you bet. You could do what you wanted to do and say anything, as long as somewhere or other, you got the story in.

"We had a gag man on those pictures. He'd give Hope a line and me a line, but I'd have no idea what he gave Hope. I'd say my line and Hope would say, 'Let's do that over,' and he'd think of one, and we'd have two good lines. They'd have the camera going pretty near all the time, even at the rehearsal.

"Something would be funny, they'd leave it in."

Dorothy Lamour, the saronged beauty of the Road pictures, played only a guest bit in the last one.

During the forties, Bing filmed *Birth of the Blues*, one of his favorites, with Mary Martin, and *Holiday Inn*, with Fred Astaire, in which he introduced the famous and well-loved song, "White Christmas," by Irving Berlin. The song went on to become the best-selling recording of a single for all time.

In 1944, he did what is probably his most popular and perhaps his best movie: *Going My Way*. Crosby established the heart-warming role of Father O'Malley, the Catholic priest who helps an elderly pastor, played by Barry Fitzgerald. A sentimental tale, to be sure, but a darling one.

In his autobiography, Crosby recalls the only Academy Award he ever won:

"Gary Cooper was chosen to hand me the award. I don't remember what he said, but when he managed to put the idea over to me that I won, a great warm feeling came over me. I stumbled up on the stage like a zombie.

"Neither Coop nor I said much. I asked, 'Are you talking about me?' And he said, 'Yup.'"

Director Leo McCarey had apparently recognized the quality in Crosby that went deeper than what had appeared in his light and musical comedies—an ability that blended talent with a warmness that was hard to match on screen. In 1945, Crosby and McCarey did an encore: *The Bells of St. Mary's*. Crosby again put on white collar as Father O'Malley, this time teaming with Ingrid Bergman.

This decade of film-making included

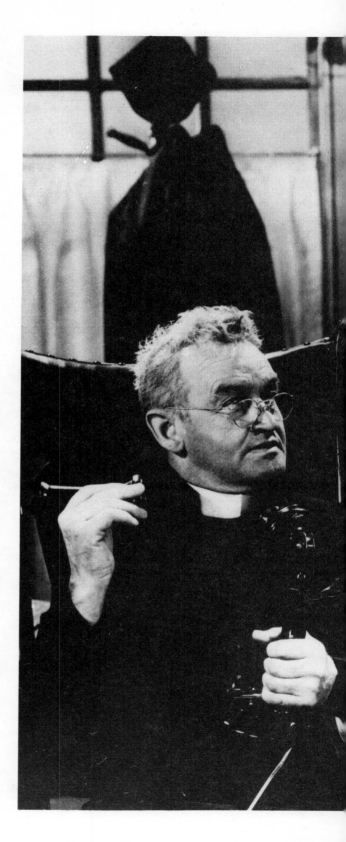

Bing points an admonitory finger at Barry Fitzgerald in "Going My Way" 1944.

"Riding High" (Paramount, 1950): Bing has some fun with costar Coleen Gray.

---

three more Road films as well as *Blue Skies* with Fred Astaire (1946); *Welcome Stranger* with Barry Fitzgerald (1947); *The Emperor Waltz* (1948—a Billy Wilder film); *A Connecticut Yankee in King Arthur's Court* (1949). Bing inaugurated the fifties with

---

"Blue Skies" (Paramount, 1946): A bit of the dialogue between Bing and Fred Astaire.

Riding High (1950), a Frank Capra movie dealing with another Crosby love (horse racing), and *Mr. Music* (1950), loaded with guest appearances and musical acts.

In 1954, Crosby made the film that proved that he was indeed an actor, and had gotten better and better at his craft since *Going My Way*. It was *The Country Girl*.

The role of a broken-down alcoholic musical comedy star was not at first one of his favorites. He once said:

mance as his suffering wife; William Holden is the stage director who tries to mold him back into shape.

Crosby got an Oscar nomination for his efforts, but lost out to Marlon Brando's *On the Waterfront*.

Director George Seaton said at the time:

"Bing doesn't enthuse easily, but I've never seen him so hepped up about anything as he is about this [*The Country Girl*].

"Bing is an excellent actor, much better than people realize. It wouldn't surprise me to see him tackle *Hamlet* some day."

Seaton had directed Crosby in another dramatic role the year before. It was in *Little*

On the set of "Mr. Music" in Hollywood, 1949, Bing chats with Nancy Olsen.

Dorothy Lamour congratulates Bing at a Paramount Studios luncheon where disc jockeys from all over the world saluted him as "Mr. Music," 1951.

"I was driving along in the car with Mona Freeman when I told her, 'I'm going to tell (director George) Seaton to get Frank Sinatra. He's hot now.' Mona told me, 'If you do, I'll never speak to you again.'"

Luckily for audiences, he took the role. *The Country Girl* is from the play by Clifford Odets. Crosby played the part created by Paul Kelly on Broadway and portrayed by Robert Young on the road. The character is that of a faded, alcoholic stage star who has one last chance to regain theatrical fame. Grace Kelly won an Oscar for her perfor-

"A Connecticut Yankee in King Arthur's Court" (Paramount, 1949): with Rhonda Fleming.

Boy Lost, a tender tearjerker in which Crosby, a former war correspondent, returns to find the son, born during World War II, whom he has never seen. Seaton was sure Crosby could carry it off (he did) and was all for leaving songs out of the film altogether. But the Paramount front office feared audience reaction to a Crosby film without the Crosby singing voice, and Johnny Burke and Jimmy Van Heusen were once more called in to write the music.

In 1955, Bing marked his fiftieth film: *Anything Goes.* It was a remake of a 1936 film with Ethel Merman and Victor Moore, but only the title—and the Cole Porter songs—remained; cast and plot differed. It is memorable in that it reunited Bing with Donald O'Connor. They had last appeared together in *Sing You Sinners* in 1937.

Crosby himself, however, had often said that his favorite film was *High Society* (1956), in which he costarred with Grace Kelly and

"The Emperor Waltz" (Paramount, 1948): Bing
enjoys a dance with Joan Fontaine.

"Mr. Music" (Paramount, 1950): Bing as "Mr.
Music" himself.

"The Country Girl" (Paramount, 1954): Grace Kelly, Bing, and William Holden. Bing got an Oscar nomination for his dramatic portrayal in this film.

Frank Sinatra. It was a remake of *The Philadelphia Story*, with music by Cole Porter.

Crosby told an AP interviewer in 1973:

"My first 25 years in show business, I was just having a good time. I loved what I was doing with good actors and musicians. It never seemed like I had any goal or anything."

"Later on, I tried to get into some good

"Little Boy Lost" (Paramount, 1953): Bing, in one of his more dramatic film efforts, with Nicole Maurey.

things. I tried to diversify and play different characters.

"Some were nice little musicals. Your favorites are things that you might have been good in or accepted as good in, like *The Country Girl, High Society, White Christmas, Holiday Inn.*"

Bing got involved with numerous other things—his family, television, golf, horse racing and such—and movies took a mezzanine, if not a back seat.

He played in *Man on Fire* with Inger Stevens and E.G. Marshall, a non-musical, somewhat melodramatic story about a man with a custody problem concerning his son and divorced wife; *Say One for Me*, in which he is a priest (again) with Sammy Cahn–Jimmy Van Heusen music; and supporting roles in *Let's Make Love* (Yves Montand and Marilyn Monroe); *High Time* (Tuesday Weld and Fabian), and *Pepe*, (Cantinflas and thirty-five others in cameo appearances) and *Robin and the Seven Hoods* (Robin Hood in Prohibition Chicago).

His last feature was *Stagecoach*, an all-star remake of the John Ford–John Wayne Western (which was better).

Significantly, Crosby and Hope wanted to make one more Road picture; one final film together. It would have reunited them with Dorothy Lamour in that affectionate association that began in 1940 with *Road to Singapore*.

"We're working on *The Road to the Fountain of Youth*," Bob Hope said in an interview before Crosby's death. "It'll be with Bing and Dorothy Lamour."

The Road to the Fountain of Youth was to be a spoof of all past Road pictures and was to have been made in England in the spring of 1978.

But, Bing, unfortunately for us all, took another road.

"High Society" (Paramount, 1956): In his favorite scene in his favorite movie, Bing sings "True Love" to Grace Kelly.

"High Society" (Paramount, 1956): Frank Sinatra and Bing toast with tuneful tones.

The versatility of Bing Crosby is shown in various movie roles he played over the years. From left: in 1938 in "Sing You Sinners"; in 1944 in

Starring and Supporting Roles

KING OF JAZZ. Universal 1930. Directed by John Murray Anderson. **Cast:** Paul Whiteman and his orchestra; John Boles, Laura LaPlante, Janette Loff, Glenn Tryon, Merna Kennedy, the Brox sisters. Crosby sang "Music Has Charms" over the credits

and The Rhythm Boys had four songs, including "So the Bluebirds and the Blackbirds Got Together."

CHECK AND DOUBLE CHECK. RKO 1930. Directed by Melville Brown. Story, music, and lyrics by Bert Kalmar and Harry Ruby. **Cast:** Amos 'n Andy, Sue Carol. The Rhythm Boys sang "Three Little Words" with Duke Ellington's Orchestra.

THE BIG BROADCAST. Paramount

"Going My Way"; in 1948 in "A Connecticut Yankee in King Arthur's Court", and in 1966 in "Stagecoach".

1932. Directed by Frank Tuttle. Screenplay by George Marion, Jr. from the play *Wild Waves* by William Ford Manley. Songs by Ralph Rainger and Leo Robin. **Cast:** Stuart Erwin, Leila Hyams, plus radio guests Burns and Allen, Kate Smith, The Mills Brothers, The Boswell Sisters, Arthur Tracy, Cab Calloway. Crosby is a crooner on the radio station of penniless George Burns; the station is "saved" when millionaire Erwin produces an all-star "big broadcast."

COLLEGE HUMOR. Paramount 1933. Directed by Wesley Ruggles. Screenplay by Dean Fales. Songs by Sam Coslow and Arthur Johnston. **Cast:** Jack Oakie, Richard Arlen, Burns and Allen. Crosby plays a singing drama professor in a campus story.

TOO MUCH HARMONY. Paramount 1933. Directed by Edward Sutherland. Screenplay by Joseph Mankiewicz and

"Going My Way" (Paramount, 1944): Bing in
his Oscar-winning role as the parish priest,
with Jean Heather and Barry Fitzgerald.

Harry Ruskin. Songs by Sam Coslow and
Arthur Johnston. **Cast:** Jack Oakie, Skeets
Gallagher, Judith Allen. Crosby works up a
small-town vaudeville act which takes him
back to Broadway.

    GOING HOLLYWOOD. Cosmopolitan–
M-G-M 1933. Directed by Raoul Walsh.
Screenplay by Donald Ogden Stewart from
a story by Frances Marion. Songs by Arthur
Freed and Nacio Herb Brown. **Cast:** Marion
Davies, Fifi D'Orsay, Stuart Erwin, Ned

Sparks, Patsy Kelly. Davies plays a French
teacher who falls in love with radio crooner
Crosby and follows him to Hollywood and
stardom.

    WE'RE NOT DRESSING. Paramount
1934. Directed by Norman Taurog. Screen-
play by Benjamin Glazer, from J.M. Barrie's
The Admirable Crichton. Songs by Harry
Revel and Mack Gordon. **Cast:** Carole
Lombard, Burns and Allen, Leon Errol, Ethel
Merman, Ray Milland. Crosby is a singing

deck hand on a beached yacht.

SHE LOVES ME NOT. Paramount 1934. Directed by Elliott Nugent. Screenplay by Benjamin Glazer from a play by Howard Lindsay, from a novel by Edward Hope. Songs by Harry Revel and Mack Gordon. **Cast:** Miriam Hopkins, Kitty Carlisle, Edward Nugent. Crosby and Nugent, Princeton undergraduates, hide showgirl Hopkins in murder mystery.

HERE IS MY HEART. Paramount 1934. Directed by Frank Tuttle. Screenplay by Edwin Justus Mayer and Harlan Thompson, from the play *The Grand Duchess and the Waiter,* by Alfred Savoir. Songs by Ralph Rainger and Leo Robin and Lewis Gensler. **Cast:** Kitty Carlisle, Roland Young, Akim Tamiroff, William Frawley, Reginald Owen, Alison Skipworth. Millionaire radio crooner Crosby meets poor European princess

"Welcome Stranger" (Paramount, 1947): Barry Fitzgerald and Bing team up again.

In "Birth of the Blues" (1941), Bing plays the clarinet while Harry Barris (of The Rhythm Boys), Perry Botkin (Bing's longtime guitarist), Mary Martin, and Brian Donlevy listen.

Carlisle and poses as a hotel waiter. Eventually, he buys the hotel and marries her.

MISSISSIPPI. Paramount 1935. Directed by Edward Sutherland. Screenplay by Francis Martin and Jack Cunningham, from an adaptation of Booth Tarkington's *Magnolia* by Herbert Fields and Claude Binyon. **Cast:** W.C. Fields, Joan Bennett, Gail Patrick. Crosby, fleeing fiancée Patrick, joins troupe on Fields's showboat, becomes known as "The Singing Killer" and returns

"Here Come the Waves" (1944), a film made during World War II.

to wed Bennett, sister of former fiancée.

TWO FOR TONIGHT. Paramount 1935. Directed by Frank Tuttle. Screenplay by George Marion Jr. and Jane Storm, from the play by Max Lief and J.O. Lief. Songs by Harry Revel and Mack Gordon. **Cast:** Joan Bennett, Mary Boland, Lynne Overman, Thelma Todd. Songwriter Crosby poses as playwright and must turn out complete musical comedy in a week.

THE BIG BROADCAST OF 1936. Paramount 1935. Directed by Norman Taurog. Screenplay by Walter DeLeon, Francis Martin, Ralph Spense. Songs by Ralph Rainger and Leo Robin, Dorothy Parker and

This dancing trio teams Bing with Virginia Dale and Fred Astaire in "Holiday Inn" 1942.

Richard Whiting, Mack Gordon and Harry Revel. **Cast:** Jack Oakie, Burns and Allen, Wendy Barrie, Akim Tamiroff, with specialties by Ethel Merman, Amos 'n Andy, Mary Boland, Charlie Ruggles, Bill Robinson, Ina Ray Hutton. Crosby sings "I Wished on the Moon."

ANYTHING GOES. Paramount 1936.

Directed by Lewis Milestone. Adapted from the musical comedy by Lindsay and Crouse. Songs by Cole Porter, by Edward Heyman and Hoagy Carmichael, by Leo Robin and Richard Whiting, by Leo Robin and Frederick Hollander. **Cast:** Ethel Merman, Ida Lupino, Charlie Ruggles, Grace Bradley, Arthur Treacher, Margaret Dumont. Crosby tries to rescue the supposedly kidnapped Lupino aboard ship, posing as a public enemy.

RHYTHM ON THE RANGE. Paramount 1936. Directed by Norman Taurog. Screenplay by Walter DeLeon, Francis Martin, Sidney Salkow, John Moffett, from a story by Mervin Houser. **Cast:** Frances Farmer, Bob Burns, Martha Raye. Crosby, a rodeo cowboy, meets debutante Farmer, who is fleeing her heiress-aunt and, when she decides to stay on range, he marries her.

PENNIES FROM HEAVEN. Columbia 1936. Directed by Norman McLeod. Screenplay by Jo Swerling, from the story, "The Peacock Feather" by Katharine Leslie Moore. Songs by Arthur Johnston and Johnny Burke. **Cast:** Madge Evans, Edith Fellows, Donald Meek, Louis Armstrong. Crosby delivers letter from condemned murderer to victim's family and winds up marrying social worker Evans and adopting 10-year-old Fellows and granddad Meek.

WAIKIKI WEDDING. Paramount 1937. Directed by Frank Tuttle. Screenplay by Frank Butler, Don Hartman, Walter DeLeon, Francis Martin from a story by Butler and Hartman. Songs by Ralph Rainger and Leo Robin, and by Harry Owens. **Cast:** Shirley Ross, Bob Burns, Martha Raye, Anthony Quinn, Grady Sutton. Publicist Crosby, to convince contest-winner Ross of Hawaii's glories, has natives kidnap everybody.

DOUBLE OR NOTHING. Paramount 1937. Directed by Theodore Reed. Screenplay by Charles Lederer, Erwin Gesley, John Moffitt, Duke Atterberry, from a story by M. Coates Webster. Songs by Arthur Johnston and Johnny Burke, Sam Coslow and Al Siegal, Burton Lane and Ralph Reed. **Cast:** Mary Carlisle, Martha Raye, Andy Devine, William Frawley. Crosby solves the freak problem of doubling a $5,000 inheritance in thirty days, and wins socialite Carlisle, too.

DR. RHYTHM. Major Pictures-Paramount 1938. Directed by Frank Tuttle.

Screenplay by Jo Swerling and Richard Connell, from an O. Henry story, "The Badge of Policeman O'Roon." Songs by Johnny Burke and James Monaco. **Cast:** Mary Carlisle, Bea Lillie, Andy Devine, Rufe Davis, Laura Hope Crews, Fred Keating, Sterling Holloway, Louis Armstrong, Franklin Pangborn. Doctor Crosby subs as bodyguard for heiress Carlisle in home of her aunt (Lillie) who is trying to prevent her niece's elopement.

SING YOU SINNERS. Paramount 1938. Directed by Wesley Ruggles. Screenplay by Claude Binyon from his own story. Songs by Johnny Burke and James Monaco, Frank Loesser and Hoagy Carmichael. **Cast:** Fred MacMurray, Ellen Drew, Donald O'Connor. Brothers Crosby and O'Connor form a singing act while training a horse for a race. They win and give up racing for singing so MacMurray can marry Drew.

PARIS HONEYMOON. Paramount 1939. Directed by Frank Tuttle. Screenplay by Frank Butler and Don Hartman, from a story by Angela Sherwood. Songs by Ralph Rainger and Leo Robin, Spencer Williams and Roger Graham. **Cast:** Akim Tamiroff, Shirley Ross, Franciska Gaal, Edward Everett Horton, Ben Blue. Millionaire cowboy Crosby seeks honeymoon castle in France for his intended bride, Ross, but falls for peasant girl (Gaal) who works in Tamiroff's tavern.

EAST SIDE OF HEAVEN. Universal 1939. Directed by David Butler. Screenplay by William Conselman, from a story by David Butler and Herbert Polesie. Songs by Johnny Burke and James Monaco. **Cast:** Joan Blondell, Mischa Auer, Irene Hervey, C. Aubrey Smith. Singing cab driver Crosby has child thrust upon him by its mother (Hervey). He and fiancée Blondell reunite child with millionaire grandfather (Smith), who sponsors radio show with Crosby.

THE STAR MAKER. Paramount 1939. Directed by Roy Del Ruth. Screenplay by Frank Butler, Don Hartman, and Arthur

Caesar, from a story by Caesar and William Pierce. **Cast:** Louise Campbell, Linda Ware, Ned Sparks, Janet Waldo, Laura Hope Crews, Walter Damrosch, Thurston Hall, Billy Gilbert. Based loosely on the career of Gus Edwards.

ROAD TO SINGAPORE. Paramount 1940. Directed by Victor Schertzinger. Screenplay by Frank Butler and Don Hartman, from a story by Harry Hervey. Songs by Johnny Burke and James Monaco, Burke and Schertzinger. **Cast:** Bob Hope, Dorothy Lamour, Anthony Quinn, Charles Coburn, Jerry Colonna, Judith Barrett. Crosby hops a freighter to avoid marrying Barrett, accompanied by Hope. They are hidden by Lamour to protect them from baddies in the jungles of a South Sea island.

IF I HAD MY WAY. Universal 1940. Directed by David Butler. Screenplay by William Conselman and Joseph Kern, from a story by Butler, Conselman, and Kern. Songs by Johnny Burke and James Monaco. **Cast:** Gloria Jean, Charles Winninger, El Brendel, Allyn Joslyn, Donald Woods. Singing steelworker Crosby helps orphan Jean locate her ex-vaudevillian grand-uncle, Winninger, who opens a nightclub.

RHYTHM ON THE RIVER. Paramount 1940. Directed by Victor Schertzinger. Screenplay by Dwight Taylor from a story by Billy Wilder and Jacques Thery. Songs by James Monaco and Johnny Burke, Burke and Schertzinger. **Cast:** Mary Martin, Basil Rathbone, Oscar Levant, Charles Grapewin, William Frawley, Phyllis Kennedy, Jeanne Cagney, Harry Barris, John Scott Trotter, Wingy Manone. Crosby and Martin, ghost songwriters for Rathbone, try to make it on their own, but audiences believe the songs are Rathbone's.

A romantic moment for Marjorie Reynolds and Bing in "Dixie" 1943.

ROAD TO ZANZIBAR. Paramount 1941. Directed by Victor Schertzinger. Screenplay by Frank Butler and Don Hartman, from a story by Hartman and Sy Bartlett. Songs by Johnny Burke and Jimmy Van Heusen. **Cast:** Bob Hope, Dorothy Lamour, Una Merkel, Eric Blore, Iris Adrian, Douglas Dumbrille, Joan Marsh, Leo Gorcey. Crosby and Hope, carnival performers stranded in Africa, try to unload fake diamond mine sold to them by Blore, but are bilked by Merkel into "buying" Lamour from slave traders.

BIRTH OF THE BLUES. Paramount 1941. Directed by Victor Schertzinger. Screenplay by Harry Tugend and Walter DeLeon from a story by Tugend. **Cast:** Mary Martin, Brian Donlevy, Eddie Anderson, J. Carrol Naish, Carolyn Lee, Ruby Elzy, Harry Barris, Jack Teagarden and Orchestra. Singer—jazz-clarinetist Crosby forms a white band to popularize jazz in pseudo-documentary blues anthology.

HOLIDAY INN. Paramount 1942. Directed by Mark Sandrich. Screenplay by Claude Binyon, from an adaptation by Elmer Rice of an original idea of Irving Berlin. Songs by Irving Berlin. **Cast:** Fred Astaire, Marjorie Reynolds, Virginia Dale, Walter Abel, Louise Beavers. Crosby and Astaire turn New England farm into nightclub open only on holidays; Crosby introduces "White Christmas."

ROAD TO MOROCCO. Paramount 1942. Directed by David Butler. Screenplay by Frank Butler and Don Hartman. Songs by Johnny Burke and Jimmy Van Heusen. **Cast:** Bob Hope, Dorothy Lamour, Anthony Quinn, Mikhail Rasumny, Vladimir Sokoloff, Monte Blue, Donna Drake, Yvonne De Carlo. Crosby and Hope, shipwrecked, swim to Morocco, where Crosby sells his friend into slavery and sets his sights on princess Lamour.

STAR-SPANGLED RHYTHM. Paramount 1942. Directed by George Marshall. Screenplay by Harry Tugend. Songs by Harold Arlen and Johnny Mercer. **Cast:** Eddie Bracken, Betty Hutton, Victor Moore, Anne Revere, Cass Daley. Hutton arranges for Moore, actually the gatekeeper, to appear to be the Paramount production chief, in an effort to impress son Bracken, who is in the Navy. All Paramount stars put in appearance, with Crosby singing "Old Glory."

DIXIE. Paramount 1943. Directed by Edward Sutherland. Screenplay by Karl Tunberg and Darrell Ware, from adaptation by Claude Binyon of the William Rankin story. Songs by Jimmy Van Heusen and Johnny Burke. **Cast:** Dorothy Lamour, Marjorie Reynolds, Billy De Wolfe, Lynne Overman, Eddie Foy, Jr. Crosby stars as Dan Emmett in fictional biography of original "Virginia Minstrels" man and author of "Dixie."

GOING MY WAY. Paramount 1944. Directed by Leo McCarey. Screenplay by Frank Butler and Frank Cavett, from a story by Leo McCarey. Songs by Johnny Burke and Jimmy Van Heusen. **Cast:** Barry Fitzgerald, Rise Stevens, James Brown, Jean Heather, Frank McHugh, Gene Lockhart, Stanley Clements, Porter Hall, Fortunio Bonanova, Robert Mitchell Boys' Choir. Crosby, in his Oscar-winning role as Father O'Malley, a progressive priest sent to help out pastor Fitzgerald in a poor parish.

HERE COME THE WAVES. Paramount 1944. Directed by Mark Sandrich. Screenplay by Allan Scott, Ken Englund, and Zion Myers. Songs by Harold Arlen and Johnny Mercer. **Cast:** Betty Hutton, Sonny Tufts, Ann Doran, Gwen Crawford. Sailors Crosby and Tufts meet Wave twins (Hutton).

DUFFY'S TAVERN. Paramount 1945. Directed by Hal Walker. Screenplay by Melvin Frank and Norman Panama. Songs by Jimmy Van Heusen and Johnny Burke, Ben Raleigh and Bernie Wayne. **Cast:** Ed Gardner, Charlie Cantor, Barry Sullivan, Victor Moore. Crosby among Paramount stars in screen version of popular radio show; Crosby sings "Swinging on a Star" with Betty Hutton, Sonny Tufts, Diana Lynn, Billy De Wolfe, Cass Daley, Howard da Silva.

"Road to Utopia" (Paramount, 1946): Bing and Bob give Dorothy Lamour the eye.

THE BELLS OF ST. MARY'S. Rainbow—RKO 1945. Directed by Leo McCarey. Screenplay by Dudley Nichols. Songs by Johnny Burke and Jimmy Van Heusen. **Cast:** Ingrid Bergman, Henry Travers, William Gargan, Martha Sleeper, Ruth Donnelly, Rhys Williams, Dickie Tyler, Una O'Connor. Crosby, in repeat of Father O'Malley role, aids a failing parochial school and arranges for transfer to a milder climate for nun Berg-man, unwitting victim of tuberculosis.

ROAD TO UTOPIA. Paramount 1946. Directed by Hal Walker. Screenplay by Melvin Frank and Norman Panama. Songs by Johnny Burke and Jimmy Van Heusen. **Cast:** Bob Hope, Dorothy Lamour, Hillary Brooke, Douglas Dumbrille, Jack LaRue. Vaudevillians Crosby and Hope wander into a gold rush, steal a map of a mine and, with dancing girl Lamour, outwit baddies.

"Blue Skies" (Paramount, 1946): Little Karolyn Kay Grimes snuggles up to Bing in the Irving Berlin musical.

BLUE SKIES. Paramount 1946. Directed by Stuart Heisler. Screenplay by Arthur Sheekman, from an Allan Scott adaptation of Irving Berlin idea. Songs by Irving Berlin. **Cast:** Fred Astaire, Joan Caulfield, Billy De Wolfe, Olga San Juan, Frank Faylen. Singing nightclub owner Crosby and dancer-turned-commentator Astaire compete for chorus girl Caulfield.

WELCOME STRANGER. Paramount 1947. Directed by Elliott Nugent. Screenplay by Arthur Sheekman from a story by Frank Butler. Songs by Jimmy Van Heusen and Johnny Burke. **Cast:** Joan Caulfield, Barry Fitzgerald, Wanda Hendrix, Frank Faylen, Percy Kilbride. Young doctor Crosby takes over practice of vacationing Fitzgerald and saves old doctor's life with help of school teacher Caulfield.

VARIETY GIRL. Paramount 1947. Directed by George Marshall. Screenplay by Edmund Hartmann, Frank Tashlin, Robert Welch and Monte Brice. Songs by Jimmy Van Heusen and Johnny Burke, and by Frank Loesser. **Cast:** Mary Hatcher, Olga San Juan, DeForrest Kelly, William Demarest, Frank

Faylen. Paramount stars pay tribute to Variety Clubs of America; Crosby and Hope do golfing scene and sing new song, "Harmony."

ROAD TO RIO. Paramount 1948. Directed by Norman McLeod. Screenplay by Edmund Beloin and Jack Rose. Songs by Johnny Burke and Jimmy Van Heusen. **Cast:** Bob Hope, Dorothy Lamour, Andrews Sisters, Jerry Colonna, Frank Faylen, Gale Sondergaard. Carnival musicians Crosby and Hope, stowaways on liner to Rio, meet heiress Lamour.

THE EMPEROR WALTZ. Paramount 1948. Directed by Billy Wilder. Screenplay by Charles Brackett and Billy Wilder. **Cast:** Joan Fontaine, Roland Culver, Lucille Watson, Richard Haydn. Crosby, as gramophone salesman, tries to sell one to Emperor Franz Josef (Haydn) and to woo Austrian countess (Fontaine).

A CONNECTICUT YANKEE IN KING ARTHUR'S COURT. Paramount 1949. Directed by Tay Garnett. Screenplay by Edmund Beloin, from the Mark Twain book. Songs by Johnny Burke and Jimmy Van Heusen. **Cast:** Rhonda Fleming, William Bendix, Cedric Hardwicke. Crosby plays Twain's Hartford blacksmith at Camelot.

TOP O' THE MORNING. Paramount 1949. Directed by David Miller. Screenplay

"Top o' the Morning" (Paramount, 1949): Bing with Barry Fitzgerald and Hume Cronyn.

by Edmund Beloin and Richard Breen. Songs by Jimmy Van Heusen and Johnny Burke. **Cast:** Ann Blyth, Barry Fitzgerald, Hume Cronyn. Insurance investigator Crosby poses as singing artist and goes to Ireland to recover stolen Blarney Stone, falling in love with Fitzgerald's daughter, Blyth.

RIDING HIGH. Paramount 1950. Directed by Frank Capra. Screenplay by Robert Riskin, Melville Shavelson and Jack Rose, from Mark Hellinger's story, "Broadway Bill." Songs by Johnny Burke and Jimmy Van Heusen. **Cast:** Coleen Gray, Frances Gifford, Charles Bickford, William Demarest. Crosby, engaged to Gifford, forsakes job with her father to train a horse, which wins big race and dies. Crosby then falls for younger sister, Gray, gets two new horses and begins again.

MR. MUSIC. Paramount 1950. Directed by Richard Haydn. Screenplay by Arthur Sheekman, from play *Accent on Youth,* by Samson Raphaelson. Songs by Johnny Burke and Jimmy Van Heusen. **Cast:** Nancy Olson, Charles Coburn, Ruth Hussey, Robert Stack, Tom Ewell. Crosby, in debt after giving up songwriting for golf, gets advance from producer-friend Coburn, who hires Olson to make sure that he keeps writing. When Coburn runs into money troubles, Crosby helps stage show at a college.

HERE COMES THE GROOM. Paramount 1951. Directed by Frank Capra. Screenplay by Virginia Van Upp, Liam O'Brien and Myles Connolly, from a story by Robert Riskin and Liam O'Brien. Songs by Johnny Mercer and Hoagy Carmichael, and by Jay Livingston and Ray Evans. **Cast:** Jane Wyman, Franchot Tone, Alexis Smith, James Barton, Anna Maria Alberghetti, Robert Keith. Crosby, a reporter, must marry within five days to keep two war orphans. Old sweetheart Wyman, tired of waiting, about to wed Tone, but Crosby breaks it up in time.

JUST FOR YOU. Paramount 1952. Directed by Elliott Nugent. Screenplay by

Robert Carson from story, "Famous," by Stephen Vincent Benet. Songs by Harry Warren and Leo Robin. **Cast:** Jane Wyman, Ethel Barrymore, Natalie Wood, Robert Arthur, Regis Toomey. Songwriter Crosby vies with son Arthur for Broadway star Wyman, while trying to get daughter Wood into finishing school run by Barrymore. Crosby gets Wyman, daughter enrolls, son writes hit song.

ROAD TO BALI. Paramount 1953. Directed by Hal Walker. Screenplay by Frank Butler, Hal Kanter and William Morrow, from story by Butler and Harry Tugend. Songs by Johnny Burke and Jimmy Van Heusen. **Cast:** Bob Hope, Dorothy Lamour, Murvyn Vye, Ralph Moody, Peter Coe, Leon Askin, Bob Crosby, Jane Russell, Dean Martin, Jerry Lewis. (First color "Road" picture.) Vaudevillians Crosby and Hope dive for sunken treasure and end up in Bali, where Crosby winds up with Lamour and Russell.

LITTLE BOY LOST. Paramount 1953. Directed by George Seaton. Screenplay by Seaton from story by Margharita Laski. Songs by Johnny Burke and Jimmy Van Heusen. **Cast:** Claude Dauphin, Nicole Maurey, Christian Fourcade, Gabrielle Dorziat, Collette Dereal. Crosby, an American journalist, returns to France to find young son who vanished during the war.

WHITE CHRISTMAS. Paramount 1954. Directed by Michael Curtiz. Screenplay by Norman Krasna, Melvin Frank and Norman Panama. Songs by Irving Berlin. **Cast:** Danny Kaye, Rosemary Clooney, Vera-Ellen, Dean Jagger, Barrie Chase. Army buddies Crosby and Kaye make it in show biz, aid sister act Clooney and Vera-Ellen and help their old

---

"Here Comes the Groom" (Paramount, 1951): Bing costarred with Jane Wyman and Franchot Tone.

"White Christmas" (Paramount, 1954): That's Rosemary Clooney at the piano, getting a little help from Bing, with Vera-Ellen and Danny Kaye.

general Jagger promote his ski lodge.

THE COUNTRY GIRL. Paramount 1954. Directed by George Seaton. Screenplay by Seaton, from the play by Clifford Odets. Songs by Ira Gershwin and Harold Arlen. **Cast:** Grace Kelly, William Holden, Anthony Ross, Gene Reynolds. Musical comedy star Crosby, wallowing in self-pity, has chance to make a comeback. Wife Kelly helps get him the break with producer Holden. (Academy Award nomination for Crosby; Academy Award for Kelly.)

ANYTHING GOES. Paramount 1956. Directed by Robert Lewis. Screenplay by Sidney Sheldon, from the play by Guy Bolton and P.G. Wodehouse. Songs by Cole Porter, Sammy Cahn, and Jimmy Van Heusen. **Cast:** Donald O'Connor, Mitzi Gaynor, Phil Harris, Kurt Kasznar, Jeanmaire, Richard Erdman. Crosby is aging matinee idol who teams up for a Broadway show with young television star O'Connor.

HIGH SOCIETY. M-G-M 1956. Directed by Charles Walters. Screenplay by John

Patrick, from *The Philadelphia Story*, by Philip Barry. Songs by Cole Porter. **Cast:** Grace Kelly, Celeste Holm, Frank Sinatra, Sidney Blackmer, John Lund, Louis Calhern, Louis Armstrong. Crosby tries to win back ex-wife Kelly, who is about to be remarried, and gets help from reporters Sinatra and Holm.

MAN ON FIRE. M-G-M 1957. Directed by Ronald MacDougall. Screenplay by Ronald MacDougall, from story by Malvin Ward and Jack Jacobs. Songs by Sammy Fain and

Danny Kaye talks with Bing on the set of "White Christmas" as director Michael Curtiz looks on. Both costarred in the film, 1954.

"High Time" (Twentieth Century–Fox, 1960):
Richard Beymer seems to have some doubts
about the unusually costumed Bing.

Paul Francis Webster. **Cast:** Inger Stevens, E.G. Marshall, Mary Fickett, Malcolm Brodrick, Anne Seymour, Richard Eastham. Crosby sings title song in story of his fight to maintain custody of son he reared after divorce.

SAY ONE FOR ME. 20th Century-Fox 1959. Directed by Frank Tashlin. Screenplay by Robert O'Brien. Songs by Sammy Cahn and Jimmy Van Heusen. **Cast:** Debbie Reynolds, Robert Wagner, Frank McHugh, Ray Walston, Les Tremayne. Crosby plays a priest in a show-business parish, protecting Reynolds, daughter of ailing friend, when she takes a job as a chorus-girl.

LET'S MAKE LOVE. 20th Century-Fox 1960. Directed by George Cukor. Screenplay by Norman Krasna. Songs by Sammy Cahn and Jimmy Van Heusen. **Cast:** Marilyn Monroe, Yves Montand, Tony Randall, Frankie Vaughan, Wilfrid Hyde–White, David Burns, Michael David, Milton Berle, Gene Kelly. Crosby sings "Incurably Romantic," while trying to teach Montand to sing.

HIGH TIME. 20th Century-Fox 1960. Directed by Blake Edwards. Screenplay by Tom and Frank Waldman, from a story by Garson Kanin. Songs by Henry Mancini, Sammy Cahn and Jimmy Van Heusen. **Cast:**

Tuesday Weld, Fabian, Nicole Maurey, Richard Beymer. Wealthy widower Crosby returns to college to complete his education and falls for French teacher Maurey.

PEPE. Columbia 1960. Directed by George Sidney. Screenplay by Dorothy Kingsley and Claude Binyon, from a story by Leonard Spigelgass and Sonya Levien. **Cast:** Cantinflas, Dan Dailey, Shirley Jones, Edward G. Robinson, Ernie Kovacs, William Demarest, and thirty-five guest stars. Crosby is one of the stars Mexican ranch hand Cantinflas meets when he follows a prize stallion to Hollywood.

ROAD TO HONG KONG. United Artists 1962. Directed by Norman Panama. Screenplay by Norman Panama and Melvin Frank. Songs by Sammy Cahn and Jimmy Van Heusen. **Cast:** Bob Hope, Joan Collins, Dorothy Lamour, Robert Morley, Peter Sellers, Frank Sinatra, Dean Martin. Dancers Crosby and Hope, with guest bit appearance by Lamour, get involved in international intrigue involving a rocket-fuel formula.

ROBIN AND THE SEVEN HOODS. Warner Bros. 1964. Directed by Gordon Douglas. Screenplay by David Schwartz. Songs by Sammy Cahn and Jimmy Van Heusen. **Cast:** Frank Sinatra, Dean Martin, Barbara Rush, Sammy Davis, Jr., Peter Falk, Edward G. Robinson, Victor Buono, Phil Crosby. Crosby is Allen A. Dale in Robin Hood story reset in Prohibition Chicago.

STAGECOACH. 20th Century-Fox 1966. Directed by Gordon Douglas. Screenplay by

Bing in his last feature film, "Stagecoach" with Slim Pickens, 1966.

Joseph Landon, based on Dudley Nichols' screenplay from Ernest Haycox story, "Stage to Lordsburg." **Cast:** Ann-Margret, Red Buttons, Michael Connors, Alex Cord, Bob Cummings, Van Heflin, Slim Pickens. Crosby plays alcoholic medic in remake of 1939 John Ford movie.

Shorts

RIPSTITCH THE TAILOR. Pathé 1930. Directed by Raymond McCarey. (Never released.)

TWO PLUS FOURS. Pathé 1930. Directed by Raymond McCarey.

I SURRENDER DEAR. Educational 1931. Directed by Mack Sennett.

ONE MORE CHANCE. Educational 1931. Directed by Mack Sennett.

DREAM HOUSE. Educational 1932. Directed by Del Lord.

BILLBOARD GIRL. Educational 1932. Directed by Mack Sennett.

BLUE OF THE NIGHT. Educational 1933. Directed by Leslie Pearce.

SING, BING, SING. Educational 1933. Directed by Babe Stafford.

STAR NIGHT AT THE COCOANUT GROVE. M-G-M 1933.

PLEASE. Paramount 1933. Directed by Arvid Gillstrom.

JUST AN ECHO. Paramount 1934. Directed by Arvid Gillstrom.

SWING WITH BING. Universal 1937.

DON'T HOOK NOW. Paramount 1938.

ANGELS OF MERCY. Metrotone News (for the Red Cross) 1941.

THE ROAD TO VICTORY. Warner Bros. (for War Activities Committee) 1941.

ALL-STAR BOND RALLY. 20th Century-Fox 1945. (Crosby sang "Buy, Buy Bonds.")

HOLLYWOOD VICTORY CARAVAN. Paramount 1945. Crosby sings "We've Got Another Bond to Buy."

BING PRESENTS ORESTE. Paramount 1956. Crosby introduces opera singer Oreste.

SHOWDOWN AT ULCER GULCH. 1958. Promotional film for the *Saturday Evening Post.*

BING CROSBY'S WASHINGTON STATE. Cinecrest 1968. Crosby narrates documentary trip around Washington.

Narration and Songs

REACHING FOR THE MOON. United Artists 1931. Crosby sings Irving Berlin's "When the Folks High Up Do the Mean Low Down."

CONFESSIONS OF A COED. Paramount 1931. Crosby, off-camera, sings "Just One More Chance."

OUT OF THIS WORLD. Paramount 1945. Crosby is the voice of singing telegraph messenger Eddie Bracken.

THE ADVENTURES OF ICHABOD AND MR. TOAD. Disney–RKO 1949. Crosby sings three Don Raye–Gene DePaul songs and narrates along with Basil Rathbone in this full-length cartoon.

CINERAMA'S RUSSIAN ADVENTURE. Cinerama 1966. Crosby narrates Soviet documentary as part of a U.S. State Department cultural exchange program.

Guest and Cameo Appearances

MY FAVORITE BLONDE. Paramount 1942.

HIGHER AND HIGHER. Paramount 1943.

THE PRINCESS AND THE PIRATE. RKO 1944.

MY FAVORITE BRUNETTE. Paramount 1947.

ANGELS IN THE OUTFIELD. MGM 1951.

THE GREATEST SHOW ON EARTH. Paramount 1952.

SON OF PALEFACE. Paramount 1952.

SCARED STIFF. Paramount 1953.

ALIAS JESSE JAMES. United Artists 1959.

"Road to Hong Kong" (United Artists, 1962): Bob Hope and Bing plant kisses on a happy Dorothy Lamour.

Bing's Greatest Hits

by Mary Campbell

Introduction

One of Edward R. Murrow's "I Can Hear It Now" records, taking a nostalgic look at popular music of the late 1920s, noted Rudy Vallee's prominence and heralded the arrival of "a husky voice from Spokane." Critic Henry Pleasants said, "He had one of the loveliest voices I have heard in forty-five years of listening to baritones, both classical and popular."

Paul Whiteman hired Bing Crosby, the possessor of that husky voice—lightly husky, with a very smooth delivery, the gentle style called crooning. Whiteman also hired Crosby's partner Al Rinker to join his band's dozen vocalists in late 1926. When their contract with the Metropolitan Theater in Los Angeles expired, Crosby and Rinker joined Whiteman at the Tivoli Theater in Chicago. But before they left Los Angeles, they cut their first record. Don Clark, band leader at the Biltmore Hotel, invited them to sing with his band and they did a duet, on October 10, 1926, recording "I've Got the Girl."

In Chicago everyone liked them. Whiteman let Crosby solo sometimes; the first time on a record was "Muddy Water." One of the next was "My Blue Heaven." When the Whiteman Orchestra opened at the Paramount Theater in New York, Crosby and Rinker were not received so well—they figured out later that they couldn't be heard without amplification in a theatre much larger than they were used to—the management asked that they be dropped from the show. Whiteman had to pay them, though, since they were under contract, and when he heard Harry Barris doing a single act, nice and loud, he put him together with Crosby and Rinker as "Paul Whiteman's Rhythm Boys," the first time a trio had sung with a band.

Rinker and Barris played miniature pianos while they sang, and Crosby beat a small cymbal.

In a holiday costume for "Bing Crosby and the Sounds of Christmas," seen on TV in December 1971, Bing gets into the Yuletide spirit.

Harry Barris (left), Bing, and Al Rinker made up the early singing trio known as The Rhythm Boys.

Barris, who was to write a number of Bing Crosby's hits, co-wrote "Mississippi Mud" in 1927. The Rhythm Boys recorded. it in a snappy arrangement in 1928 and of all the records they made it is probably the best remembered. (You can hear some good Bix Beiderbecke licks on it, too.)

"Mississippi Mud" was a forerunner of what would become a typical "Crosby song"—what would now be called "laid-back" lyrics, nothing tense, not sophisticated, but pleasant, pleasurable, friends and neighbors having a simple good time. Crosby sang that kind of song during the Depression, but he also had sung it earlier, during the prosperity of the Coolidge years.

On the back of that record was "From Monday On," a tune Barris and Crosby wrote together. *Show Boat* had opened on Broadway in December 1927, so in 1928 Crosby also recorded "Ol' Man River," backed by "Make Believe" from that score. The usual approach to "Ol' Man River" was melodrama. Bing's approach, predictably, was not. His singing was relaxed, even swinging, overcoming Whiteman's fast, bouncy tempo.

Crosby's records sold right from the first. He wasn't the first crooner to come along and he didn't do everything right on records from the very start, but he certainly had a mellifluous voice. Some people made fun of his "blubbery crooning" but most people liked it—a lot.

Crosby's best range was B flat to B flat, but apparently he didn't know that. In his early years of recording, he often sang—as in "Ol' Man River"—a lot higher. Above B flat, his voice lost the special sound which identified it as Crosby and became an unexceptional tenor. However, one thing he did was to ease back in volume as he approached top notes, because he realized his baritone had a thin top—and he did this in an era of tenors, who thought it was a sign of virility to increase volume as they hit the high notes, ringing out a "big finish."

The Rhythm Boys left Whiteman's Orchestra in 1929. They recorded "I'll Get By" as the Ipana Troubadours, and "Three Little Words" with the Duke Ellington Orchestra. Those were the days in which Ellington recorded music by other composers besides himself and the vocal group he had originally hired for "Three Little Words" couldn't hack it. Ellington's orchestra always was geared to the instrumentalists, making it hard for singers to work with. The Rhythm Boys filled in on the "Three Little Words" recording session and later that year sang the song with the Ellington Orchestra again—in blackface—in the movie *Check and Double Check.*

Also in 1930, Crosby recorded "My Kinda Love" with the Dorsey Brothers. Ray McKinley, who was the drummer with the Dorsey Brothers Orchestra from 1934 to 1935 said, "The emphasis on the trombones was to give the band a Bing Crosby quality. The Dorseys often played for Bing and they felt that they could achieve some relationship if they pitched their sound like his."

The Rhythm Boys, late in 1930, joined Gus Arnheim, who had the top West Coast orchestra of the late 1920s and early 1930s, ensconced at the Cocoanut Grove in Los Angeles. "It Must Be True" and "Wrap Your Troubles in Dreams," both by Barris, were sung by Crosby in 1930 and 1931. They're the first two records on which, to lend variety, Crosby whistles—and, in true jazz fashion, he stays away from the melody.

Singing with the trio, Bing had learned to sing lightly and with the forward projection essential to distinct enunciation. In 1931, his brother Everett sent his new Arnheim record of "I Surrender, Dear"—Bing's first big solo hit record—to NBC and CBS radio in New York. CBS hired him and he started his first show, on September 2, 1931, with "Just One More Chance." He was pushing another new record. On the same show he sang "I'm Through with Love," which he also recorded that year. That song was co-written by Matty Malneck, violinist in the Whiteman orchestra.

Bing crooned traditional "suitor" effortlessly, but the love song which was the radio show's theme told the joys of marriage and family, "My Blue Heaven."

Bing, now out on his own as a soloist, was deprived of the jazz arrangements the trio had been using. He moved closer to the mainstream of popular music and he fell back on influences of his first singer model, Al Jolson. He slurred like Jolson, though more musically, earning him the tag "the Groaner." The slurs gradually became a light, fast, attractive "catch" in the voice. That can be heard on nearly every Crosby track that exists.

In 1931, Crosby collaborated on writing a song, not so different in theme from "My Blue Heaven," which would become a theme song. He wrote "Where the Blue of the Night Meets the Gold of the Day" with a couple of New Yorkers—Fred E. Ahlert and Roy Turk. Presumably, the "boo-boo-boos" between the mellow phrases were Bing's idea.

Crosby's career didn't start on the radio—though for many listeners it seemed to be the case. It started in public halls and he had to learn to use the microphone to enhance the best of his voice—unstrained, with the microphone adding volume. He became a

It's melody time as Bing sings with The Andrews Sisters (LaVerne, Patty, and Maxine) during a Hollywood recording session, 1943.

master of words, treating them affectionately, casually, gaily, but, as he said himself, he didn't start out that way. Jazz critic George Simon said, "He was blessed with a naturally warm voice—deep, resonant, appealing. He learned how to phrase with it almost by osmosis. He was the best, and he was also the most natural."

Critic Pleasants said, "Bing's most original contribution was the lowering of the voice, not so much in pitch as in intensity, to a conversational level." But Pleasants agrees with Crosby's own disparaging assessment of the carelessness of his early recordings. "In the 1930s he sang badly and the records sold.

But it was not, I think, just the casual, relaxed phrasing that sold them. The records sold because of the beautiful sound of the voice."

In 1932, Crosby recorded the Depression's theme song, "Brother, Can You Spare a Dime?" and the more cheerful "Happy-Go-Lucky You." The next year brought more optimism, with "I've Got the World on a String," and the mellow serenity of "Down the Old Ox Road." And Crosby, the lyricist, went to work again. With composer Victor Young, he and lyricist Ned Washington collaborated on "A Ghost of a Chance." In 1934, he recorded "Love in Bloom," from a picture he was in, *She Loves Me Not*.

By 1935, when the big bands were taking over, ushering in the era of swing, Bing Crosby was the leading popular singer in the world.

By the late 1930s, Crosby's style had changed from romantic, emotional crooning to a light, airy style. The arrangements by John Scott Trotter, his musical director on radio and records, and songs by Johnny Burke and Jimmy Van Heusen—writing songs for the "Road" pictures—fitted the new mood very well.

In 1936, Crosby made one of his biggest hit records, "Pennies from Heaven," by Arthur Johnston and Burke, the title song from a movie which also included his old friend, Louis Armstrong. That song's lyrics were perfectly suited for the Depression.

Lyricist Sammy Cahn has said, "You didn't write a Bing Crosby song. You wrote a song and when he sang it, it became a Bing Crosby song." Well, maybe, but there were unifying threads running through the songs he chose to record. Crosby sang songs that made people feel good about themselves.

Jack Benny and Bing dance along with George Burns (1954).

Bing "The Groaner" Crosby lends an ear to Frank "The Voice" Sinatra as they discuss Sinatra's appearance on Bing's radio show, 1944.

The people in his songs were friendly, downright neighborly, kind, with graceful personalities, at peace with themselves. They weren't losers, didn't carry the torch, weren't embroiled in high-powered drama, weren't money-hungry, clawing their way to the top. Instead, they gathered in the cool, cool of the evening when the party's gettin' a glow on and singing fills the air. They watched April play the fiddle, baked a sunshine cake, went fishin'.

Americans take their popular song lyrics seriously and the ones that speak closest to their hearts become standards. Lyrically

Crosby's records weren't all escapes from reality. Some were about the reality of a person's better, upbeat side, the side he wanted himself to be, and was encouraged by Bing Crosby's words that Bing was and he also could be.

In 1934, Decca Records signed Bing Crosby, the new company's first artist. On August 8, 1934, Bing cut his first record for Decca, where the bulk of his life's recordings would be made. Most of the earlier ones had been on Brunswick.

Jack Kapp, the head of Decca Records, didn't much like the boo-boo-boos and he was instrumental in getting Bing gradually to drop them. He also wanted to make sure that Bing wasn't typecast and he suggested all kinds of songs. The fact that Bing sang so many—some say he sang 4,000 different songs in his lifetime—was partly due to Kapp. In 1936, Crosby recorded a couple of gently Western songs written that year, "I'm an Old Cowhand" and "Twilight on the Trail" as well as "The Way You Look Tonight" and "A Fine Romance" as a duet with his wife, Dixie Lee.

Jerome Kern's "The Folks Who Live on the Hill," was a Crosby record release of 1937. Composer Alex Wilder thinks it was less Kern's melody and more Oscar Hammerstein's "Edgar Guestian homespun lyrics" which impressed the fans. Crosby also recorded bandleader Harry Owens' paean to his infant daughter, "Sweet Leilani," which won the Academy Award that year.

Metronome magazine picked three of Bing's records as among the thirty-eight best records of 1937. They were "I Never Realized," termed "the prettiest Bing singing of the year," "Peckin'," "a heap of fun and swing with the Jimmy Dorsey band," and "Bob White," "ditto with Connee Boswell."

One "Crosby song" followed another, with charm and nonchalance. A 1938 record was "I've Got a Pocketful of Dreams," 1939 brought "Go Fly a Kite," and 1940, "April Plays the Fiddle" and the Academy Award song "When You Wish upon a Star."

Crosby introduced many songs in movies; he then recorded them, to each song's lasting fame. In 1942, he recorded "White Christmas," from the movie *Holiday Inn*. It was such a big hit that he recorded it twice again—in 1946, when it was in *Blue Skies*, and 1954, when it was the title song for *White Christmas*. Many people think "White Christmas" is Crosby's best-selling record but he claimed that distinction for "Silent Night," with "Adeste Fideles" on the back. "White Christmas," however, was one of

With Mary Martin, Bing sings "White Christmas" during the shooting of ABC-TV's first color spectacular, shown on Christmas Eve, 1962.

the first five songs voted into the National Academy of Recording Arts and Science's "Recording Hall of Fame" when that institution was founded in 1974.

Oklahoma! had opened on Broadway in 1943 and Crosby warbled "People Will Say We're in Love" and "Oh, What a Beautiful Morning" into the recording microphone. Record hits from Crosby's 1944 picture *Going My Way* were "Swinging on a Star," (which won the Academy Award),

"Going My Way" and the lullaby, "Too-Ra-Loo-Ra-Loo-Ral."

The next year, *Here Come the Waves* produced a dynamic Harold Arlen–Johnny Mercer number that mothers told their children to pay attention to and some listeners took as Bing Crosby's philosophy of life: "Ac-Cent-Tchu-Ate the Positive." Another part of his lifestyle was underscored the same year, when he recorded Cole Porter's "Don't Fence Me In."

"Aren't You Glad You're You?" in 1945 was from *Bells of St. Mary's* and Harry Warren and Johnny Mercer's "On the Atchison, Topeka & Santa Fe," from *The Harvey Girls*, which Bing wasn't in, won the Acad-

emy Award. In 1946 he recorded "Personality" from *Road to Utopia* and "Day by Day," the song that caused Doris Kappelhoff to change her last name—to Doris Day.

"In the Cool, Cool, Cool of the Evening" won the Academy Award in 1951 and Crosby, of course, who sang it in *Here Comes the Groom*, recorded it. One of the songs he recorded from the 1954 film, *White Christmas* was the gentle but lyrically upbeat "Count Your Blessings Instead of Sheep."

In 1956, when Elvis Presley burst on the American music scene, bringing rock 'n' roll as the fiery tail of his comet, the thirty-third best-selling single record of the year was "True Love," a duet by Bing and Grace Kelly.

Their annual TV Christmas special, in 1971 titled "Bing Crosby and the Sounds of Christmas," brought carolers Harry, Kathryn, Bing, **Mary Frances, and Nathaniel into the living rooms of America.**

Long-time friend Bob Hope has just handed
Bing the "Crummy Award," during the taping
of Crosby's TV special, March 1977.

Host Bing smilingly gives his attention to
guest star Dean Martin on Bing's second
musical variety special of the 1969-70 season,
"Bing Crosby, Cooling It," seen on NBC-TV
in April 1970.

Presley's "Don't Be Cruel" topped the list.
With rock, Crosby's recording schedule
slowed down. When he cut records, they
were LPs, and they weren't too frequent.
In 1968, the year after the movie, *Thoroughly Modern Millie*, he made an LP named
"Thoroughly Modern." He recorded "Bing
'n' Basie" in 1973 and the critic in *Stereo
Review* magazine said, "After the advent

Frank Sinatra and Bob Hope break up at the sight of John Wayne singing with Bing. The scene took place during the taping of a TV special in 1975.

of Crosby, singers stopped singing at you, like Jolson, and started singing to you, like Bing." Crosby said that year he thought it might be his last recording session. But it wasn't.

In 1973, British TV made a 14-part series about Crosby's life. It stirred up so much interest in him there that he recorded and brought out—not an LP aimed at the older folks—but a single, which sells to the young market. That final single, which Crosby thought would not interest Americans (so it

Mary Frances Crosby and her father sing a duet during a taping of his TV special, "Bing," March 1977.

wasn't released in the United States) was "Tie a Yellow Ribbon 'Round the Old Oak Tree" and "It's Not Where You Start, It's Where You Finish" from Broadway's *Seesaw*.

In 1976, he made two LPs in England, which were released in America. One was "Feels Good, Feels Right" and one, with Crosby one of four writers of the title song, was "That's What Life Is All About."

Critic George Simon wrote, before Bing Crosby's death, "Though his singing gained polish and maturity through his half a century of recording, it never lost the ease and charm and musical enthusiasm and honesty that in themselves reflect so accurately the man himself."

Bob Hope and Bing celebrated their thirtieth year in entertainment together when Bing did a guest stint on Hope's NBC-TV special, October 1962. Their comedy sketch was a takeoff on "Bonanza," with Crosby as Adam Cartwright and Hope as Little Joe.

Longtime buddies Crosby and Hope make a 1971 joint appearance on NBC-TV's "Chrysler Presents the Bob Hope Special."

Bing and Kathryn headline a Christmas show for their eighth straight year for 500 aged and infirm residents of San Francisco's city-run Laguna Honda Nursing Home, 1975. Crosby told them, "You can see it's a special occasion; I even wore my hair."

Bing and Kathryn rehearse for his television special, March 1977.

Bing rehearses for his TV special, March 1977.

His Greatest Hits

1926 I've Got the Girl (Bing Crosby and Al Rinker)—with Don Clark's Orchestra

1927 Muddy Water — with Paul Whiteman's Orchestra
Side By Side/Pretty Lips (The Rhythm Boys)—with Paul Whiteman's Orchestra
My Blue Heaven—with Paul Whiteman's Orchestra
Magnolia (The Rhythm Boys)—with Paul Whiteman's Orchestra

1928 That's Grandma/Wa Da Da, (Paul Whiteman's Rhythm Boys)—with Paul Whiteman's Orchestra
I'm Winging Home—with Paul Whiteman's Orchestra
Ol' Man River/Make Believe—with Paul Whiteman's Orchestra
From Monday On/What Price Lyrics? (Paul Whiteman's Rhythm Boys)—with Paul Whiteman's Orchestra
Mississippi Mud (The Rhythm Boys)—with Paul Whiteman's Orchestra
'Taint So Honey, 'Taint So—with Paul Whiteman's Orchestra

Perry Como rehearses a duet with Bing for an ABC-TV special, 1950.

I'm Afraid of You, My Pet—with Paul Whiteman's Orchestra

1929 Louise/So the Bluebirds and the Blackbirds Got Together (Paul Whiteman's Rhythm Boys)

Makin' Whoopee—with Paul Whiteman's Orchestra

Waiting at the End of the Road—with Paul Whiteman's Orchestra

Great Day/Without a Song—with Paul Whiteman's Orchestra

(I'm a Dreamer) Aren't We All/If I Had a Talking Picture of You—with Paul Whiteman's Orchestra

My Kinda Love/Till We Meet

I Kiss Your Hand, Madame/Baby, Oh Where Can You Be?—with Paul Whiteman's Orchestra

I'll Get By/Rose of Mandalay (Ipana Troubadours)

My Kinda Love—with the Dorsey Brothers and their Orchestra

1930 A Bench in the Park (The Rhythm Boys and The Brox Sisters)—with Paul Whiteman's Orchestra

A Bench in the Park (Paul Whiteman's Rhythm Boys)

It Must Be True/Fool Me Some More—with Gus Arnheim's Orchestra

Happy Feet (The Rhythm Boys)—with Paul Whiteman's Orchestra

I Like To Do Things for You (The Rhythm Boys)—with Paul Whiteman's Orchestra

Three Little Words (The Rhythm Boys)—with Duke Ellington's Orchestra

Song of the Dawn—with Paul Whiteman's Orchestra

1931 Just a Gigolo/Wrap Your Troubles in Dreams

Just One More Chance/Were You Sincere?

I'm Through with Love/I Found a Million Dollar Baby

With the almost ever-present pipe, Bing poses at Paramount Studios, 1942.

At Your Command/Many Happy Returns of the Day

Prisoner of Love

Where the Blue of the Night Meets the Gold of the Day/I'm Sorry Dear

I Surrender Dear—with Gus Arnheim's Orchestra

Ho-Hum/I'm Gonna Get You—with Gus Arnheim's Orchestra
Dinah—with the Mills Brothers
One More Time/Thanks to You—with Gus Arnheim's Orchestra

1932 Lazy Days/Happy-Go-Lucky You
Love, You Funny Thing/My Woman
Here Lies Love/How Deep Is the Ocean?
Please/Waltzing in a Dream—with Anson Weeks's Orchestra
Let's Put Out the Lights/Brother, Can You Spare a Dime?

1933 You're Getting To Be a Habit with Me/I'm Young and Healthy
Just an Echo in the Valley
I've Got the World on a String/Linger a Little Longer
Temptation/We'll Make Hay While the Sun Shines
Learn To Croon/Moonstruck—with Jimmie Grier's Orchestra
After Sundown/Beautiful Girl
Down the Old Ox Road/Blue Prelude—with Jimmie Grier's Orchestra
Thanks/Black Moonlight—with Jimmie Grier's Orchestra
The Day You Came Along/I Guess It Had To Be that Way—with Jimmie Grier's Orchestra
A Ghost of a Chance

1934 Love in Bloom/Straight from the Shoulder—with Irving Aaronson and his Commanders
I'm Hummin', I'm Whistlin', I'm Singin'—with Irving Aaronson and his Commanders
Love Thy Neighbor/Ridin' Around in the Rain—with Nat W. Finston's Paramount Orchestra
Beautiful Girl—with Lennie Hayton's Orchestra
Once in a Blue Moon—with Nat W. Finston's Paramount Orchestra

Good-night, Lovely Little Lady—with Nat W. Finston's Paramount Orchestra
May I?—with Nat W. Finston's Paramount Orchestra
She Reminds Me of You—with Jimmie Grier's Orchestra
I Love You Truly/Just A-Wearyin' for You
After Sundown—with Lennie Hayton's Orchestra
We'll Make Hay While the Sun Shines—with Lennie Hayton's Orchestra
Temptation—with Lennie Hayton's Orchestra
Our Big Love Scene—with Lennie Hayton's Orchestra
The Moon Was Yellow/The Very Thought of You
May I?/She Reminds Me of You

Bing belts out a Christmas tune, joined by Kathryn and their three children, Nathaniel, 7, Mary Frances, 9, and Harry Lillis, 11, during the taping of their annual appearance on the Hollywood Palace TV Christmas show, 1968.

1935 June in January/Love Is Just Around the Corner

With Every Breath I Take/Maybe I'm Wrong Again

It's Easy to Remember/Swanee River

Soon/Down by the River

I Wished on the Moon/Two for To-night

I Wish I Were Aladdin/From the Top of your Head

Without a Word of Warning/Takes Two to Make a Bargain

1936 Pennies from Heaven/Let's Call a Heart a Heart

Would You?/Lovely Lady

Twilight on the Trail/The Touch of Your Lips

Robins and Roses/We'll Rest at the End of the Trail

Empty Saddles/Roundup Lullaby

I'm an Old Cowhand/I Can't Escape from You

A Fine Romance/The Way You Look Tonight (with Dixie Lee Crosby)

1937 Sweet Leilani

I Never Realized

What Will I Tell My Heart?/Too Marvelous for Words

The Moon Got in my Eyes/Smarty

It's the Natural Thing To Do/All You Want To Do Is Dance

The Folks Who Live on the Hill/Can I Forget You?

Peckin'—with the Jimmy Dorsey Orchestra

Bob White (with Connee Boswell)

1938 I've Got a Pocketful of Dreams/A Blues Serenade

My Heart Is Taking Lessons/On the Sentimental Side

My Reverie/Old Folks

Now It Can Be Told/It's the Dreamer in Me

I Have Eyes/The Funny Old Hills

1939 It Must Be True/I Surrender Dear

Bette Midler, dressed as a CBS usher, and Bing rehearse for his television special, "Bing," March 1977.

East Side of Heaven/Sing a Song of Sunbeams

A Man and his Dream/Go Fly a Kite

Yodelin' Jive (with The Andrews Sisters)

1940 When You Wish upon a Star

Can't Get Indiana off my Mind/I Found a Million Dollar Baby

The Singing Hills/Devil May Care

Only Forever/The Moon over Madison Square

That's for Me/Rhythm on the River

April Played the Fiddle/I Haven't Time To Be a Millionaire

Pearl Bailey breaks up during a duet with Bing. They were rehearsing for his TV special, March 1977.

Put It There, Pal/The Road to Morocco (with Bob Hope)

1943 I'll Be Home for Christmas/Danny Boy—with John Scott Trotter and his Orchestra

If You Please/Sunday, Monday or Always—with The Ken Darby Singers

People Will Say We're in Love/Oh, What a Beautiful Morning—with Trudy Erwin and The Sportsmen Glee Club

Poinciana/San Fernando Valley—John Scott Trotter and his Orchestra

Pistol Packin' Mama (with The Andrews Sisters)

1944 Going My Way/Swinging on a Star

Too-Ra-Loo-Ra-Loo-Ral/I'll Remember April—John Scott Trotter and his Orchestra

It Could Happen to You/The Day after Forever

Amor/Long Ago and Far Away

Sleigh Ride in July/Like Someone in Love

Strange Music/More and More

There's a Fellow Waitin' in Poughkeepsie/Ac-Cent-Tchu-Ate the Positive,—with Vic Schoen and his Orchestra

Mairzy Doats

Don't Fence Me In (with The Andrews Sisters)

1945 If I Loved You/Close as Pages in a Book

A Friend of Yours/All Of My Life—with John Scott Trotter and his Orchestra

I'd Rather Be Me/On the Atchison, Topeka & Santa Fe—with John Scott Trotter and his Orchestra

Out of this World/June Comes Around Every Year—with John Scott Trotter and his Orchestra

Aren't You Glad You're You?/In the Land of Beginning Again—with John Scott Trotter and his Orchestra

1941 It's Always You/You Lucky People You

Shepherd Serenade/The Anniversary Waltz

Tea for Two/Yes, Indeed—with Connee Boswell and Bob Crosby's Bobcats

1942 White Christmas/Let's Start the New Year Right

Skylark/Blue Shadows with White Gardenias

Lamplighter's Serenade/Mandy Is Two

Happy Holiday/Be Careful, It's my Heart

Moonlight Becomes You/Constantly

1946 Day By Day/Prove It by the Things You Do

Personality/Would You?—with the Eddie Condon Orchestra/with John Scott Trotter and his Orchestra

White Christmas—with John Scott Trotter, his Orchestra, and chorus

1947 My Heart Is a Hobo/Country Style

You Do/How Soon?

Ballerina/Golden Earrings—with The Rhythmaires and John Scott Trotter and his Orchestra

But Beautiful/One I Love—Victor Young and his Orchestra/John Scott Trotter and his Orchestra

Now Is the Hour/Silver Threads Among the Gold—with the Ken Darby Singers

Galway Bay/My Gal's an Irish Girl—with Victor Young and his Orchestra

Y'All Come/Changing Partners—with the Cass County Boys and the Perry Botkin Orchestra/with Jud Conlon's Rhythmaires and the Perry Botkin Orchestra

Tallahassee/Go West, Young Man (with The Andrews Sisters)

Connecticut/Mine (with Judy Garland)—with Joseph Lilley and his Orchestra.

1948 Careless Hands/Memories

1949 So in Love/Why Can't You Behave?—Vic Shoen and his Orchestra

Dear Hearts and Gentle People/Mule Train—with Jud Conlon's Rhythmaires and the Perry Botkin Orchestra/with the Perry Botkin Orchestra

The Four Winds and the Seven Seas

1950 Sunshine Cake/The Horse Told Me—accompanied by the Jeff Alexander Chorus with Victor Young and his Orchestra

A Marshmallow World/Looks Like a Cold, Cold Winter—with the Lee Gordon Singers and Sonny Burke and his Orchestra

Beyond the Reef/Harbor Lights—with Lyn Murry and his Orchestra

High on the List/Life Is So Peculiar (with The Andrews Sisters)—with Vic Shoen and his Orchestra

Gone Fishin' (with Louis Armstrong)

Sam's Song/Play a Simple Melody (with Gary Crosby)

1951 In the Cool, Cool, Cool of the Evening

1954 Count Your Blessings Instead of Sheep

White Christmas/God Rest Ye Merry Gentlemen—with The Ken Darby Singers and John Scott Trotter and his Orchestra/with Max Terr's Mixed Chorus and John Scott Trotter and his Orchestra

1956 You're Sensational

True Love (with Grace Kelly)/Well Did You Evah (with Frank Sinatra)

Bing and Kathryn dance during the taping of a TV special, "Bing," a salute to his 50 years in show business, March 1977.